M

DATE DUE

MAY 2 7 2004	
AUG 3 – 2004	
SEP 0 2 2004	

MAR 1 8 2004

Remember
Me
When
I'm
Gone

Remember
Me
When
I'm
Gone

LARRY KING

NAN A. TALESE
Doubleday
NEW YORK LONDON TORONTO SYDNEY AUCKLAND

PUBLISHED BY NAN A. TALESE
AN IMPRINT OF DOUBLEDAY
a division of Random House, Inc.
1745 Broadway, New York, NY 10019

DOUBLEDAY is a registered trademark of Random House, Inc.

Library of Congress Cataloging-in-Publication Data
    Remember me when I'm gone / [compiled] by Larry King.—
1st ed.
       p.   cm.
    A collection of their own obituaries written by celebrities
themselves for Larry King, talk show host.
    1. Celebrities—Obituaries.   2. Obituaries—United States.
3. Biography—20th century.   4. King, Larry, 1933—
Interviews.   5. United States—Biography.   6. United
States—Social life and customs—20th century.   I. King,
Larry, 1933–

CT220.R46 2004
920.073'09'045—dc22
[B]

                          2003060032

ISBN 0-385-50175-7

PRINTED IN THE UNITED STATES OF AMERICA

April 2004

First Edition

10 9 8 7 6 5 4 3 2 1

CONTENTS

～∞～

When my good friend and book agent, Bill Adler, called me with the idea for this book, I was a little skeptical.

I have known Bill for more than thirty years, and we have published at least half a dozen books together—many of which were very successful—but this was his wildest idea to date.

"Why would anyone want to write their own obituary or epitaph?" I asked Bill.

And his reply was, as he usually is, very direct. "It is an opportunity for well-known people from all walks of life to let the world know how they would like to be remembered. Very few people have that opportunity."

Bill convinced me, and obviously convinced over three hundred celebrities who contributed to the book.

I think you will find this entertaining to read, certainly interesting, and very revelatory.

Larry King
Beverly Hills, CA

Curtain Call

ACTORS AND ACTRESSES

ALAN ALDA

∽∘∾

Here Lies Anonymous—Our Greatest Author.

∽∘∾

ALAN ALDA is a multi-award-winning actor, writer, and director. He first appeared on film in 1962 in *Gone Are the Days*. He is perhaps best recognized for his portrayal of wisecracking Army surgeon Benjamin Franklin "Hawkeye" Pierce in the TV series *M*A*S*H*, which ran from 1972 through 1983.

JAYNE MEADOWS ALLEN

∽∘∾

No, no, my dear ones, do not weep!
There is no cause to grieve.
For I am by his side again,
My dear beloved, Steve.

∽∘∾

JAYNE MEADOWS ALLEN is an Emmy Award–winning actress. She and her late husband, Steve Allen, were married for nearly fifty years and starred in numerous television programs together, including Steve Allen's memorable PBS miniseries, *Meeting of Minds*.

JUNE ALLYSON

❦

When I was a young girl I loved to watch Ginger Rogers dance. I would watch her over and over and eventually learned many of her dance steps.

When I went to my first audition, the steps I learned from Ginger were the ones I used. They hired me on the spot.

My advice to anyone who has a desire to be a dancer or be in the movies is to find someone they really admire, watch them and learn from them.

Success will be yours.

❦

JUNE ALLYSON is an award-winning actress, singer, and dancer. She has appeared in numerous movies including *The Stratton Story* and *The Glenn Miller Story*, co-starring James Stewart, as well as *The Girl in White* and *They Only Kill Their Masters*. She has recently appeared in various television commercials.

ED ASNER

❦

The possible conversations heard at the passing of Ed Asner:

I had no idea that in his later years he wore a bald cap!

He wrote every word that ever came out of his mouth.

He spoke of having learned his cavalry technique under Jeb Stuart sans the cavalier peccadillos of that gentleman—and later applying them to the Red Army Cavalry.

Though he spoke twenty-seven languages, he seldom had occasion to use them, perhaps because ten of them were obscure Chinese dialects.

As a child he knew Etruscan but he forgot it.

From those savants he trusted and occasionally entrusted certain confidences, it might be gathered that his rather lengthy sojourn on earth (if his figures are to be believed) was short in terms of his life and that even more astounding, his life did not commence and will not be terminated on earth. In other words we have what would be called an ET here. Opening the storage locker next to Walt Disney's may reveal that Ed Asner has left the planet. Requiescat Pacem.

∽o∾

ED ASNER is a multiple Emmy Award–winning actor. His portrayal of Lou Grant, head of the WJM newsroom on *The Mary Tyler Moore Show*, earned him three Emmys during the show's seven-season run. He also received an Emmy for his villainous appearance on the miniseries *Roots*.

MAX BAER JR.

∽o∾

Birth, Life, Death . . . Whatever

The shell of life is broken and the air of death is breathed,
A cry of being is uttered by the hand of an expertise.
The warmth and quiet gone forever, the fight and toil here.

5

How much better it would have been for all if he had
    stayed in there.

For the future holds a tiny fist that grasps and strikes the air,
But never ever wins the war, just slowly loses hair.
We enter naked, whole & pure and forever is our wish,
But we exit thus not quite the same for life is but a swish.

So come ye all to eat my fruit and share with me my lusts,
For it won't be long my brothers, before we turn to dust.

✌∾o∾

MAX BAER JR. starred as Jethro in the CBS television series *The Beverly Hillbillies*. He has gone on to write, direct, produce, and star in a wide variety of films, including *The Asphalt Cowboy* and *Hometown USA*.

BOB BALABAN

✌∾o∾

Bob's top-ten list of things he would like to be remembered by:

10. He was always late for the party, but when he got there he was a lot of fun.
 9. Balding people who wear glasses make the best pets.
 8. Never underestimate the power of the well read.

7. You can accomplish a lot by being annoying.
6. He was short, but his personality was tall.
5. Check his cell phone, he's probably got it with him.
4. He played a lot of nasty smart people, but he wasn't that nasty and he wasn't that smart.
3. He would like to posthumously thank Christopher Guest for the best time he ever had while filming anything.
2. Contrary to popular belief, *Close Encounters of the Third Kind* was not loosely based on Bob's life.
1. And the number one thing Bob would like you to remember about him: You can take the boy out of Chicago, but you can't take the Chicago out of the boy.

∾∘∾

BOB BALABAN is an actor and director who has appeared in such iconic films as *Midnight Cowboy* and *Close Encounters of the Third Kind*. He has recently paired up with actor and director Christopher Guest, appearing in two of Guest's acclaimed faux documentaries, *Waiting for Guffman* and *Best in Show*.

KAYE BALLARD

❦

As I Lay Dialing

❦

KAYE BALLARD is an actress and singer. Her first film appearance was in 1957 when she starred in *The Girl Most Likely*. She also starred in the television sitcom *The Mothers-in-Law*, produced by Desi Arnaz.

JOANNA BARNES

❦

At Last—A Parking Space!

❦

JOANNA BARNES is an actress who has appeared in such prominent films as *Home Before Dark* and *Spartacus*. In the mid-1970s, she retired from acting to pursue a second career as a novelist.

STEPHANIE BEACHAM

❦

I thank you, I love you
Please don't mourn for me
We shall all meet again
You just wait and see.

I'm leaving this body
Which has served me well,
To stay in it longer
Might start to be hell.

I've loved living this life
It has been rich and fine,
Now I'm going for a rest
With the truly Divine.

❦

STEPHANIE BEACHAM is an actress. Her breakthrough film perform-
ance came in 1972 with her portrayal of Miss Jessel in *The Nightcomers*.
She went on to hold starring roles in such prominent television series as
Dynasty and *Beverly Hills 90210*.

SHELLEY BERMAN

❦

For years I've been claiming, "I'm only human, I'm only
human." Maybe now you'll believe me.

❦

SHELLEY BERMAN is an actor, comedian, stage performer, author, and
screenwriter. He also teaches humor writing in the Master of Professional
Writing Program at the University of Southern California.

TONY BILL

❦

Forgive Me If I Don't Get Up.

❦

TONY BILL is an actor and a producer. After appearing in several films
with Frank Sinatra, including *Come Blow Your Horn, None But the Brave,*

and *Marriage on the Rocks*, he went on to produce the Academy Award–winning film *The Sting*. He made his directorial debut in 1980 with the poignant film *My Bodyguard*.

MICHAEL IAN BLACK

∽∘∾

There is much to say about the comic actor Michael Ian Black—none of it very good. He was not a kind man. Children disliked him intensely. Animals even more. Those who knew him best wished they didn't.

And yet, there was much to admire about Michael. For example, his breath was usually tolerable, his socks often matched, and his skin, while bad, almost never required serious dermatological care.

He was a survivor. Throughout his life, whenever he was faced with adversity, Michael was never known to complain. Instead, he simply cried. Through an endless succession of failed relationships and angry creditors, he persevered. And hid.

While his personal life was, at best, in shambles, it was within the professional milieu that he took his greatest pride. In the future, when we look back on the great actors of the day, we will think of Michael not at all. We will think not of the obnoxious character Phil on the NBC show *Ed*, nor of the short-lived but equally obnoxious Pets.com sock puppet, for which he provided the voice and hirsute forearm. Nor will we think of any of the other repellant characters he portrayed during this thankfully attenuated career.

And so it is with heavy heart that we bid Michael adieu. His taste in music may have been terrible, but his choice of wardrobe was worse.

∾o∾

MICHAEL IAN BLACK is an actor and comedian who has appeared in a variety of television roles. He was a cast member and script writer for the sketch comedy show *The State*, which ran for three seasons on MTV. Currently, he stars in the Emmy Award–nominated NBC television series *Ed*.

HUNT BLOCK

∾o∾

Who? Me?

∾o∾

HUNT BLOCK is an actor who stars as Craig Montgomery in *As the World Turns*. He has also appeared in the feature films *The Lonely Guy* and *The Next Best Thing*.

EDDIE BRACKEN

∾o∾

I think a quote that I stand behind is that the past, the physical past, is really a memory of today. It doesn't exist otherwise. It's just a memory. And the future never gets here. So where are we? We are only in the now. I used to try to fight my way out of things. Today, I'm not like that. I don't worry about anything. When I do start to worry, I remind myself of who I am. I've made some mistakes in my life, but I'm not ashamed of them. The mistakes you make in life add up to what you grow into. And I'm pretty proud of the guy I grew into.

❧

EDDIE BRACKEN was a singer and an actor. His first significant role was the 1940 musical comedy *Too Many Girls*. He is perhaps best remembered for his work in a pair of irreverent comedies, *The Miracle of Morgan's Creek* and *Hail the Conquering Hero*. He passed away on November 14, 2002.

BERNIE BRILLSTEIN

❧

Once I said I wanted my gravestone to read "From *Hee Haw* to *Saturday Night Live*," but it's gone far beyond that now. So maybe this: "He made a difference. He made people laugh. He made people happy. People wanted to be with him." Not now, though.

❧

BERNIE BRILLSTEIN is a producer who has worked behind the scenes in Hollywood for more than forty years. He recently produced *The Replacement Killers* starring Chow Yun Fat. He is also the author of an autobiography entitled *Where Did I Go Right?*

CHRIS BURKE

∽o∾

I would like to be remembered that I had a wonderful life. That I had my parents, family, relatives and my friends.

I would like to bring my *Life Goes On* episode videos to heaven and always be Corky for all my fans.

And remember me with smiles and laughter.

∽o∾

CHRIS BURKE is an actor and musician. He starred as Corky on the hit television series *Life Goes On*. As an actor with Down syndrome, Chris Burke has transformed America's image of the mentally and physically handicapped.

RUTH BUZZI

∽o∾

When God made me, He broke the mold. Not that anybody else'd be very interested in using it. I never had a big line of people standing around, waiting for cell samples of Ruth Buzzi to clone. My face was too long, my legs too short and my eyes too close together.

I could have been a gorgeous armadillo.

But, it isn't what you start out with that counts, is it?

When I left this earth, I hope you didn't cry for me. I would have much preferred you just popped in one of the videotapes—and had another laugh.

∽o∾

RUTH BUZZI is a comedic actress who starred for many years on the award-winning television program *Rowan and Martin's Laugh-In*.

MICHAEL CAINE

❧

See you later, no hurry.
Take good care of yourself!

❧

SIR MICHAEL CAINE is a multiple-award-winning actor. His first major film role was in 1963 when he starred in the adventure film *Zulu*. He won his first Academy Award in 1986 for his performance in *Hannah and Her Sisters* and his second in 2000 for his role in *The Cider House Rules*. He was knighted by Queen Elizabeth II in June of 2000.

DYAN CANNON

❧

She learned to listen and
her style was a smile—
even when things
weren't always worthwhile . . .

She learned to live
a life of Love
that came directly
from God above.

❧

DYAN CANNON is an award-winning actress who has starred in a wide variety of movie and television roles, including the feature film *Heaven Can Wait*. She is also the director of two films, including *The End of Innocence*, based on her autobiography.

DAVID CARUSO

✐

If my wishes were granted,
my dreams would be smashed.

✐

DAVID CARUSO is a Golden Globe Award–winning actor who starred in the hit television programs *NYPD Blue* and *Hill Street Blues*. He currently stars in *CSI: Miami*.

JOANNA CASSIDY

✐

Here lies Joanna, lady from the skies
Her laugh was as bawdy as the light in her eyes
Six feet under, what a great surprise
That life was as beautiful as one can possibly surmise.

✐

JOANNA CASSIDY is an award-winning actress. She appeared in the 1982 production of *Blade Runner*. She also starred in *Who Framed Roger Rabbit?* and has appeared in a variety of television programs, such as *Buffalo Bill*.

∽•∾

No matter how dark the moment, love and hope are always possible.

∽•∾

GEORGE CHAKIRIS is an award-winning actor who has starred in a variety of film and television roles. Following his 1961 Academy Award–winning performance in *West Side Story*, he went on to star in such highly acclaimed series as *Dallas* and *Masterpiece Theatre*.

CHEVY CHASE

∽•∾

"Anytime I cash in now, I win." That's a quotation from one of America's truly great humorists, Charles M. Russell. I use this quote because it best sums up how I feel about the remarkable luck I've had during my life: to have three incredible daughters from one even more incredible wife of more than twenty years; to have a career spanning more than twenty-five years of fame and stardom; and to love what I do (even more than the critics) is a blessing that I can't attribute to a God so much as a series of and confluence of exigencies I would call fate or luck.

My epitaph, I decided years ago, would read: "Dig him up and give him CPR." I wish to be buried in a lush daybed coffin with a phone, extra oxygen tank, a change of underwear, and an answering machine.

So my obituary should stress that the greatness I've left behind resides in my family and friends. Whatever fond or un-fond memories must be what they must be; I've had a lot of laughs.

∾○∾

CHEVY CHASE is an award-winning comedic actor who has appeared in numerous major motion pictures. An Emmy Award–winning writer and ac-tor during the first season of *Saturday Night Live* in 1975, he later starred in the comic films *Caddyshack, Fletch,* and *National Lampoon's Vacation.*

KRISTIN CHENOWETH

∾○∾

Kristin was your basic "all-American" girl, and lived life happily. She was a role model for young people, encourager to her friends, respected her brother, and loved her parents. She was a singer who felt blessed to be able to share her gift with so many people. Above all, she was a Christian who, right *now*, is rejoicing with her Lord in heaven.

∾○∾

KRISTIN CHENOWETH is an award-winning actress who has starred in several Broadway productions, including a 1999 Tony Award–winning per-formance in *You're a Good Man, Charlie Brown.*

KEVIN CONWAY

He played many characters, both dark and funny.
Won some awards, made a little money.
Great writers provided his wit and his soul.
How much was Kevin? How much the role?
His life and career became a mixed brew.
Who lies under here? I haven't a clue!

One regret though, I guess no big thing.
He never once appeared on Larry King.

KEVIN CONWAY has acted in a variety of films and television programs. He starred in *Slaughterhouse Five* and PBS's *The Scarlet Letter* and is perhaps best known for his Broadway and television portrayal of Dr. Frederick Treves in *The Elephant Man*.

CATHY LEE CROSBY

Her love, laughter, honor, caring and joy for life are as alive as ever, and will remain radiant and fully expressed in the hearts of all those whose life she touched.

*Disclaimer: The opinions expressed above do not necessarily reflect the view of Heaven, its CEO, or any affiliates thereunder.

CATHY LEE CROSBY has appeared in a wide variety of feature films, miniseries, and made-for-TV films and is also an accomplished athlete. The daughter of Linda Hayes and *Lawrence Welk Show* announcer Lou Crosby, she starred in the 1974 made-for-TV film *The New, Original Wonder Woman* and went on to co-host television's *That's Incredible*.

KATHRYN CROSBY

❦

To top the earthly
Life I've led,
Heaven will have to be
Spectacular!

❦

KATHRYN CROSBY is an actress and an author. She hosts the annual Crosby Golf Tournament in Winston-Salem, North Carolina, in honor of her late husband, Bing Crosby. She appeared on Bing's Christmas specials and on *The Kathryn Crosby Show* as well as in several Broadway productions, including *Much Ado About Nothing* and *Pygmalion*.

NORM CROSBY

❦

When as I die of age or ill,
And there I lie, stone cold and still;
When as you stare upon my shroud,

Good friends beware don't speak too loud.
For though my pulse no longer is perking,
The hearing aids might still be working.

∽∘∾

NORM CROSBY is a comedic actor who is perhaps best known for his witty malapropisms featured on *The Ed Sullivan Show*.

TED DANSON

∽∘∾

Be back in a minute.

∽∘∾

TED DANSON is a two-time Emmy Award and Golden Globe–winning actor. He starred as barkeeper Sam Malone in the beloved sitcom *Cheers* and has appeared in television and film, where his credits include *Three Men and a Baby* and *Mumford*.

ROBERT DAVI

∽∘∾

This was written in his will: If I, Robert Davi, should meet my demise before I win my Oscars, then just write on my tombstone:

In life awards are the last things on my mind. I'd rather be remembered as a great dad to my two boys Oscar and

Tony and my two beautiful little girls Emmy and Oscaretta, and of course, my pet dog, Razzy. Try the veal! I'll be here all eternity!

∽o∾

ROBERT DAVI is one of Hollywood's most beloved bad guys, having played the villain role in numerous television shows and movie features, including *Contract on Cherry Street* with Frank Sinatra and *The Goonies*. He recently starred as Merlin in *The Sorcerer's Apprentice* and did voice work on the video game Grand Theft Auto: Vice City.

LARAINE DAY

∽o∾

Coming home.

∽o∾

LARAINE DAY is an actress who has appeared in a wide variety of television programs and feature films. She starred as Nurse Mary Lamont in the *Dr. Kildare* series of movies. She is the author of two books, *Day With Giants* and *The America We Love*.

JUDI DENCH

∽o∾

She had a great sense of humour.

∽o∾

DAME JUDI DENCH is a multiple-award-winning actress who was awarded the Order of the British Empire in 1970 and made Dame of the

British Empire in 1988. She stars in the British television comedy *As Time Goes By* and has appeared in several films, including *Mrs. Brown*, *Shakespeare in Love*, and *Iris*.

JOHN DYKSTRA

∽০∾

I'm surprised at how hard it is to think of something to say about myself after I'm dead considering how much practice I had while I was alive.

∽০∾

JOHN DYKSTRA is a producer and an award-winning special and visual effects expert. He received an Academy Award in 1977 for his visual effects work in *Star Wars*. He was also nominated for an Academy Award for his work in *Stuart Little*, *Star Trek: The Motion Picture*, and *Spider-Man*.

ELVIRA

∽০∾

If they ever ask about me when I'm gone, tell 'em I was more than just a great set of boobs. I was also an incredible pair of legs.

And tell 'em I never turned down a friend. I never turned down a stranger for that matter.

And tell 'em that when all is said and done, I only ask that people remember me by two simple words . . . any two, as long as they're simple.

∽o∼

ELVIRA, also known as "Mistress of the Dark," is a Hollywood persona who has come to epitomize vamp. She has starred in numerous cult films; her alter ego, Cassandra Peterson, also appears in a number of films.

ROBERT ENGLUND

∽o∼

An actor's career ebbs and flows,
Forgotten highs, remembered lows.
Stage, movies, countless TV shows,
Remembered highs, forgotten lows.

With over sixty movies, the one you knew best
Was that horror icon from the '80s
That gave you no rest.

Quick-witted and trained,
He knew all his lines.
He liked foreign locations
And drinking fine wine.

He was on set on time,
And ready to go,
From Bucharest to Budapest,
From Stowe to Idaho.

Freddy Krueger's to blame
For endless dream kills.
And provided the world
With matinee thrills.

So here lies Robert Englund
And you know what that means.
He will wait an eternity
To wish you sweet dreams.

ROBERT ENGLUND is an actor who is perhaps best known for his terrifying portrayal of Freddy Krueger in the *Nightmare on Elm Street* series.

ROBERT EVANS

Living well is the best revenge!

ROBERT EVANS is a Hollywood producer who has brought the public such successful and award–winning films as *Chinatown* and *The Godfather*. His autobiography, *The Kid Stays in the Picture*, was recently released as a documentary film.

PETER FALK

How do I want to be remembered?

Well, that's obvious! I want to be remembered as the outstanding homicide detective who was in reality an undiscovered Picasso.

PETER FALK is a multiple Emmy Award–winning actor who is best known for his role as the title character in the hit television series *Columbo*. He won a Tony Award in 1972 for his performance in Neil Simon's comedy *The Prisoner of Second Avenue*, and has since appeared in several films, including *The Princess Bride*.

RHONDA FLEMING

❦

Here lies a Godly woman, whose caring and compassion was to help the hurting and the needy, including women, children, and animals.

❦

RHONDA FLEMING is a film, television, and stage actress who is also a well-known philanthropist and humanitarian. She has acted with many of Hollywood's leading men, including Bing Crosby, Bob Hope, and Ronald Reagan.

MILOS FORMAN

❦

I am speechless. Trust me.

❦

MILOS FORMAN is a Czechoslovakian-born filmmaker who has directed many Academy Award–winning films, including the classics *One Flew Over the Cuckoo's Nest* and *Amadeus*. His recent films include *The People vs. Larry Flynt* and *Man on the Moon*. He also served as director of Columbia University's film division.

ANTHONY FRANCIOSA

જ⌁૦

As I lie here I can't help thinking
My life has been a joke—
And it's no laughing matter.

જ⌁૦

ANTHONY FRANCIOSA is an actor who has appeared in a wide variety of films and television series as well as on stage. He received an Academy Award nomination for his performance in *A Hatful of Rain* and also starred in the television sitcom *Valentine's Day*.

BEVERLY GARLAND

જ⌁૦

Pioneering leading lady who starred in forty-one films and more than seven hundred television programs while raising four children. From 1950 to 2002 co-starred opposite Hollywood's greatest leading men and was a regular on eight TV series. In 1957 became the first actress to star in the title role of a TV dramatic series, *Decoy*. In 1983 awarded her star on Hollywood Walk of Fame. After her husband of thirty-nine years died in 1999, devoted more of her time and energy to the hotel he built and named after her, The Beverly Garland Holiday Inn in North Hollywood, CA.

જ⌁૦

BEVERLY GARLAND is an actress who has appeared in hundreds of television shows and movies, including such classics as *The Bing Crosby Show, My Three Sons,* and *Remington Steele.*

BRAD GARRETT

❀

Leave the gun, take the cannolis.
If this is heaven, where are all the strip joints?
At least I'm not in France.
Lincoln is shorter in person.
I'd rather be breathing.
Joke's over, lemme out.
What's with all the angels?
It's Sinatra's heaven, God just lives in it.

❀

BRAD GARRETT is a comedic actor who began his career as a stand-up comedian and now stars as Raymond's brother on the hit television program *Everybody Loves Raymond*. He has lent his unforgettable voice to *The Transformers*, *The Jetsons*, and *Toonsylvania*.

LARRY GELBART

❀

Having the last laugh is highly overrated.

❀

LARRY GELBART is a distinguished screenwriter and producer. He produced and wrote for the television classic *M*A*S*H* and wrote the screenplays for *A Funny Thing Happened on the Way to the Forum* (with Burt Shevelove), *Oh, God!*, and *Tootsie*.

MARLA GIBBS

❦

Our world reflects our collective consciousness. I hope that consciousness is no longer comfortable living in extreme wealth while others suffer in starvation and homelessness. That fame and fortune no longer rule the day or exploit the masses, but are seen as opportunities to share those creative gifts with others to bring hope and joy. My hope is that I will have in some way, small or large, contributed to this achievement, if only in a private, spiritual way. I'll be ready to leave thirty at last.

❦

MARLA GIBBS is an award-winning actress who starred in *The Jeffersons* and *227*.

ROBERT GOULET

❦

I will be remembered by my family and friends.
There will be sadness and some tears, but shared memories will evoke much laughter and that will make me happy.
They should discern a chortle from my urn.
My epitaph shall read: "He left them smiling!"

❦

ROBERT GOULET is an award-winning singer and performer who has appeared on Broadway and in film. He starred in the Broadway production of *Camelot* and won a Tony Award for his performance in *The Happy Time*.

SPALDING GRAY

Spalding Gray was born in 1941 in Providence, RI. He was a loving and devoted father to his two sons, Forrest and Theo, and his stepdaughter, Marissa Maier. He loved and cherished his wife, Kathleen Russo.

Most of all, Spalding will be remembered for his autobiographical monologues in which he would sit on stage at a table with a glass of water and talk for more than an hour and a half, telling true stories from his life. He was like a talking everyman because his life, although a little eccentric, was not that different from all of ours. Only he would be able to capture in such vivid detail, and highlight it with such humor, that it caused audiences both to laugh and relate.

Spalding was an American Original and the "Talking Man" will be deeply missed.

SPALDING GRAY is a performer and actor who is best known for his eloquent monologues, the most famous of which is *Swimming to Cambodia*. He co-founded the experimental Wooster Theatre Group, whose graduates include Willem Dafoe.

DOLORES HART

Remember, O Virgin Mother, when you stand in the presence of God to speak to Him of the good that is in us, that He might turn his indignation from us.

REVEREND MOTHER DOLORES HART was an actress in the 1950s, starring opposite Elvis Presley, before changing her life path and joining a Benedictine order of nuns.

TIPPI HEDREN

∽०∾

As in the true meaning of the Sanskrit word *Shambala*, she did her best to make a difference in the hope of making the world a meeting place of peace and harmony for all beings, animal and human!

∽०∾

TIPPI HEDREN is an actress who starred in the cult classic *The Birds*, directed by Alfred Hitchcock. She is the mother of actress Melanie Griffith.

MARIEL HEMINGWAY

∽०∾

Mariel lived her life in the knowledge that life is a test. She knew too well that her path brought pain as well as joy. Her aim was to observe both with equanimity. Whether or not she was successful is of no matter, as now she exists in the ever-new joy of God's love. The same love that envelops her now is guiding her family. In that knowledge there is comfort and all is well.

∽०∾

MARIEL HEMINGWAY is an actress who has starred in a variety of films. She received an Academy Award nomination for her role in Woody Allen's

Manhattan and went on to star in *Personal Best*. She is the granddaughter of Ernest Hemingway.

FLORENCE HENDERSON

∽∘∾

In the Beginning there was Faith, Hope and Love
In the End there was Faith, Hope and Love
In the Middle—I had my doubts.

∽∘∾

FLORENCE HENDERSON is an actress who starred as Carol Brady on the long-running and highly acclaimed television classic *The Brady Bunch*.

JUDD HIRSCH

∽∘∾

If this life was considered by all learned men to be the *real* one, he certainly hoped the next one would afford him a better beginning.

∽∘∾

JUDD HIRSCH is an actor who has appeared on Broadway as well as in a variety of film and television roles. He is a two-time winner of both the Emmy Award and the Tony Award. He starred as Alex Reiger in *Taxi* and received a Golden Globe Award for his performance as John Lacey in *Dear John*.

SHIRLEY JONES AND MARTY INGELS

∽o∾

Tough when you've survived 640 married years (through meditation and separation and therapy and Prozac and subpoenas and counseling and hand-to-hand combat) even your *eulogies* have to be coordinated!

> SHIRLEY JONES
> *It's been a year, my husband dear*
> *(You never were a liar)*
> *You said you'd come if I went first*
> *So where in blazes are ya?*

> MARTY INGELS
> *My Wife, my Love, my Soul Mate*
> *Promised true to follow me.*
> *And so, right near beside me here*
> *I trust there lies all three.*

∽o∾

SHIRLEY JONES and MARTY INGELS are both successful actors who have starred in a variety of films and television programs. Shirley Jones is an Academy Award–winning veteran of film and stage and also starred in the television classic *The Partridge Family*. Marty Ingels is a stand-up comedian, actor, and agent.

KATO KAELIN

∽⚬∾

I guess my fifteen minutes are up!

∽⚬∾

KATO KAELIN is America's favorite houseguest.

STACY KEACH

∽⚬∾

Here lies Stacy Keach
A Georgia peach
Lived at the beach
Now out of reach.

∽⚬∾

STACY KEACH is an actor who has appeared in such blockbuster films as
The Heart Is a Lonely Hunter and *American History X*. He also starred in the
Fox television series *Titus* and as the title role in the television series *Mike
Hammer*.

JACK KLUGMAN

❦

I hope I have left this earth without a single skeleton in my closet.

❦

JACK KLUGMAN is an actor who is perhaps best known for his Emmy Award–winning performances as Oscar Madison in the long-running hit series *The Odd Couple*.

SHIRLEY KNIGHT

❦

I am grateful that during my life I became enlightened enough to understand that violence is not a viable option. I am saddened that others were not similarly blessed.

❦

SHIRLEY KNIGHT is an accomplished actress who has appeared in a wide variety of films, television programs, and Broadway theater productions, including *Sweet Bird of Youth* opposite Paul Newman and television's *Outer Limits*.

ALAN LADD JR.

༄

Behind the quiet, humble façade Alan Ladd managed to grab two Academy Awards, raise four daughters, and play a mean game of tennis. Never one to brag, Laddie, as his friends called him, lived a full life. A devoted football fan, his year started after Labor Day and finished with the big game. He was a great humanitarian, generous with his time, money, and advice. His wife once said, "He was very conservative, except when it came to houses and movies, and then he was a riverboat gambler." Whether you knew him for a minute or a lifetime, you were always the better for it.

༄

ALAN LADD JR. is a prominent Hollywood producer who has been CEO or president of many major production companies, including Twentieth Century Fox and MGM.

DIANE LADD

༄

As you are now, I once was. Make it count.

༄

DIANE LADD is an award-winning actress who has appeared in such major motion pictures as *Chinatown* and *Wild at Heart*. She is the mother of actress Laura Dern, with whom she starred in *Rambling Rose*; the mother-daughter team made history when they both received Academy Award nominations for their work in the film.

PIPER LAURIE

✹

So far I fear I have failed to use my gifts fully.

✹

PIPER LAURIE is an actress. She received Academy Award nominations for her performances in *The Hustler, Carrie,* and *Children of a Lesser God.* She also starred in the television classic *Twin Peaks.*

CHRISTOPHER LEE

✹

As an actor I would wish to be remembered for a body of work, rather than for a few glittering years of celebrity among the pygmies of our fine profession. During my career I have met and worked with so many decent, dedicated, loyal and intelligent members of my profession, which is what *I* will remember. We are not all rogues and vagabonds. There will be nothing written on any gravestone about me: who could top Vincent Price's "I'll be back." I am content. Sometimes I feel that all this was done by somebody else. At least, I feel I could say, "He was different."

✹

CHRISTOPHER LEE is an actor who has played a breadth of characters, including Dracula in the 1958 Hammer film and Saruman the White in the *Lord of the Rings* trilogy.

JANET LEIGH

✎∽

Life is the showing forth of the very Self of God. I seldom was able to live up to that honor, but God knows I tried.

✎∽

JACK LEMMON

✎∽

Jack Lemmon. In.

✎∽

JERRY LEWIS

✎∽

How do I want to be remembered?
I don't! I really couldn't care less.
If, indeed, I am remembered after I'm gone, I won't know the difference anyway. I won't be able to hear about it, or read

about it, so my idea is this: I may open a chain of eulogy stores placed in malls, arcades, libraries, wherever there's foot traffic. And people will be able to go into the store, pay the man a small fee and have him read all the wonderful things that will be said about you once you've bought the ranch.

So with that in mind let me say, "Tell me now, not later, now, so I can enjoy it."

If all else fails, how about "This guy loved life, and the people in it."

∽o∾

JERRY LEWIS is a renowned comedic actor, famous for his slapstick comedy routines. He is also a noted philanthropist and serves as national chairman of the Muscular Dystrophy Association.

SUSAN LUCCI

∽o∾

I wish that life should not be cheap, but sacred, I wish the days to be as centuries, loaded, fragrant.
—Ralph Waldo Emerson

. . . and for me they were.

∽o∾

SUSAN LUCCI is an Emmy Award–winning actress who has starred as Erica Kane in the highly successful ABC daytime drama *All My Children* for more than thirty years. She is also the recipient of the People's Choice Award and the Soap Opera Digest Award for outstanding lead actress.

DOROTHY MALONE

≈

Dorothy Malone will be remembered as an imaginative and patient woman who excelled in every activity in which she took part. She went to Hollywood at age eighteen and worked a slow, long way to the top. She never dreamed of being famous. Yet, by following her imagination she was able to accomplish so much and support so many.

≈

DOROTHY MALONE is an actress who is best known for her big screen performances, including her Academy Award–winning role in *Written on the Wind*. She also starred in television's *Peyton Place*.

RUE McCLANAHAN

≈

See you later.

≈

RUE McCLANAHAN is an Emmy Award–winning actress who starred as Blanche Devereaux in the long-running hit series *The Golden Girls*. She also appeared in the television classics *Mama's Family*, *All in the Family*, and *Maude*.

ANN BLYTH McNULTY

❧

The Last Act. Curtain Going Up.

❧

ANN BLYTH McNULTY is an actress who has appeared on film and stage. She received an Academy Award nomination for her performance as Joan Crawford's daughter, Veda, in *Mildred Pierce* and later served as the spokeswoman for Hostess cupcakes.

KATHY NAJIMY

❧

Here lays a woman child.
A feminist-activist, never mild.
Exotic face, gardenia smell
Ashes strewn over Taco Bell.

❧

KATHY NAJIMY is an actress who has appeared in several movies and television series, including *Soapdish, The Fisher King, Sister Act*, and *Veronica's Closet*.

PATRICIA NEAL

⤳o⤸

Show me heaven! I have seen hell.

⤳o⤸

PATRICIA NEAL won an Academy Award for her role in *Hud*. She was awarded the Heart of the Year Award by President Johnson in 1968 and received a second Academy Award nomination for her performance in *The Subject Was Roses* in the same year.

NICHELLE NICHOLS

⤳o⤸

Most of you knew me as Uhura, Chief Communications Officer on the *Star Ship Enterprise* in the legendary *Star Trek* series. It was a role in which a young black actress was able to capture the hearts of the world's viewing audience by portraying a woman of color with dignity, strength, intelligence, courage and beauty. And at a time in history when Hollywood and much of the world offered more disdain than opportunity to black women who aspired to something more than servitude.

Now, if you ask *me* what my greatest accomplishments were, it would not be the aforementioned of which I'm quite proud, nor would it be that beautiful Star on the Hollywood Walk of Fame, nor even the honorary title of Living Legend, though I do admit that's cool. No, it would be the gift of motherhood to a beloved and talented son, Kyle Johnson, and having raised him to be the kind, loving and talented man he is. It would be the lifelong friendship of scientist-composer Jim

Meechan, who was the wind beneath my wings. It would be to know that somehow I lifted the lives I touched . . . to know that the blessed life I lived was justified through compassion and service to others.

Finally, I pray to be remembered as a woman who, beyond her professional abilities of acting, singing, writing and lecturing, was generous of heart with an ardent love for humankind and a deep spirituality. And if you'd like to throw in a captivating sensuality, a powerfully positive attitude, a contagious sense of humor laced with unmatched fortitude, that's all right, too!

∽○∾

NICHELLE NICHOLS is an actress who starred as Uhura in the television series *Star Trek* and in its spin-off feature films.

JOE PANTOLIANO

∽○∾

A Eulogy for Joey Pants in Rhymed Iambic Pentameter spoken by U.S. Senator Candice Pantoliano-King, A.K.A. Candy Pants, at a memorial service for her grandfather at Sinatra Park, Hoboken, New Jersey, USA, September 12, 2063:

> *God grants you life at birth, but ne'er a say*
> *In what accoutrements you'll fetch that day.*
> *Alas, that fortune's gifts can seem unkind,*
> *As Epimetheus was so assigned*
> *To grant our earthly qualities in haste,*
> *And yet, that dowry's worth is oft misplaced.*

At worst, the hand you're dealt will form a stack
Of testimonies to the things you lack,
Replete with tempting evidence to prove
The case against your competence to move
Beyond your nurtured fears and fretful caste
And leave you where we started, in your past.

At best, the hand provokes and prods you on,
A challenge to conclusions not foregone
But moldable instead, if you dare dream
And by your very will choose to redeem
The spoils of life regardless of your roots
For you, the world will not withhold its fruits.

Recall the adage, crass as it may be:
The size of your endowment's not the key,
It's what you do with it that counts the most
The echo of our dear departed host.

The witty wisdom never ceased to flow,
All wax, no wane, my winsome Grandpa Joe
Would never once allow me to forget
The stories of his youth, of how he met
His destiny across the Hudson shore,
Empowered by his choice to strive for more,
Yet tenderly beholden to the place
That gave him more than just his poker face,
That gave him his Italian-Jersey charm,
That nearly had him on the prison farm,
That taught him economics on the street,
That taught him how to thrive without conceit,
That forced him to find comfort on the stage,
That made him ever eager to engage
His family, his friends and strangers too,
In storytelling til his face turned blue.

But, through those countless anecdotes and tales,
The memories of his life, like sprightly sails,
Have whisked him past his earthly resting place,
And landed him a first-rate parking space
Precisely in the spot he treasured best.
That's right, he's in your hearts. You've been possessed.
It's better than it sounds, there's lots of perks—
You'll learn to tell the good guys from the jerks,
And know just how to mark down any price,
And find out how to add a little spice
To everything that you intend to do
Cause life's too friggin' short—to name a few.

If death is but an epilogue to life,
Its words are writ by those whose hearts are rife
With love, and there's no choice but to concede,
His legacy's our breath, the lives we lead.
That's how he always saw it from the start,
His children and their children, we'll impart
The lessons of the past as we pursue
The dreams that move us forward into who
Knows what, but that's for us to figure out.
And that is, after all, what life's about.

I'll end with Grandpa Joe's last living plea,
An epitaph that he proposed to me:
A tomb whose visits might just rival Grant's,
Here lies our dear beloved Joey Pants.

(written in collaboration with Eddie Mordujovich)

JOE PANTOLIANO, also known as Joey Pants, has appeared in several major motion pictures, including *The Matrix*. He is perhaps best known for his role on the multiple-award-winning series *The Sopranos*.

TONY RANDALL

❦

See you tomorrow.

❦

TONY RANDALL is an Emmy Award–winning television, film, and stage star. His many credits include the Broadway production of *Inherit the Wind* and television's *The Odd Couple*, in which he starred as the unforgettable Felix Unger. He created the National Actors Theater in New York in 1991.

ROB REINER

❦

Now I'm in *this* place.

❦

ROB REINER is a multi-award-winning actor and director. He received two Emmy Awards for his performance as Michael Stivic in *All in the Family* and went on to direct such classic films as *This Is Spinal Tap, Stand by Me, The Princess Bride*, and *When Harry Met Sally*. He is the co-founder of Castle Rock Productions.

DEBBIE REYNOLDS

✧

Debbie Reynolds should be remembered for her sense of humor, love of her family, devotion to her work on her motion picture museum, and her love of performing.

✧

DEBBIE REYNOLDS is an actress and dancer. After starring in the beloved musical *Singin' in the Rain*, she starred in many films and recently received praise for her role in *Mother*. She is the mother of actress Carrie Fisher.

CLIFF ROBERTSON

✧

Mea Culpa

Maybe I have crossed the Rubicon of professional concern. Maybe a cavalier recklessness has pushed aside political prudence. Or maybe, God forbid, my Calvinist conscience has presented itself front and center demanding that I, as Oliver Cromwell said, "Paint me as I am, warts and all!"

Whatever, as today's youth are wont to say. I acknowledge my warts and weaknesses while striving to overcome them.

I still hope and, yes, pray I may have left some small footprint on these vanishing sands of time. Recognizing it is no longer low tide in my life, and though the surf is rising, I still await the elusive Ninth Wave* for I will not, cannot ever, ever surrender.

That wave is the wave that is going to carry me home.

*The Ninth Wave is kind of a natural miracle. Among surfers it used to be said that the Ninth Wave was inordinately powerful, important, and a good one to ride to shore on.

∽o∾

CLIFF ROBERTSON is an Emmy Award and Academy Award–winning actor. He portrayed President Kennedy in *PT 109* and received an Academy Award for his performance in the film *Charly*.

FRED ROGERS

∽o∾

He did his best to be a thoughtful, grateful neighbor. He cared most about the deep, the simple, the quiet and the kind. He loved his family, his friends, his music and his God; and he always said that the best words in any language were *Thank you, thank you, thank you*.

®2002, Fred Rogers

∽o∾

FRED ROGERS, better known as Mr. Rogers of *Mister Rogers' Neighborhood*, hosted the children's television program for more than thirty years before his retirement in 2001. He wrote the above knowing he was very ill. He passed away on February 27, 2003.

ARNOLD SCHWARZENEGGER

∽o∾

I had fun!

∽o∾

ARNOLD SCHWARZENEGGER is an award-winning actor and body-builder. He served as chairman of the President's Council of Physical Fitness and Sports and starred in the *Terminator* series of films. He was elected governor of California in 2003.

MARTIN SHEEN

∽o∾

What I'd like to be remembered for? For about five minutes.

∽o∾

MARTIN SHEEN is an Emmy Award–winning actor who stars in the critically acclaimed television series *The West Wing*. He also starred in the motion pictures *Apocalypse Now* and *The American President* and is an ardent social and environmental activist.

AARON SPELLING

∽o∾

Stay tuned! I may be here, but my show was picked up!

∽o∾

AARON SPELLING is an award-winning actor, director, and producer who has produced classic television series such as *Dynasty, Family, Charlie's Angels*, and, more recently, *Beverly Hills 90210* and *Melrose Place*.

MAUREEN STAPLETON

∽o∾

I hope I see you later.

∽o∾

MAUREEN STAPLETON is an actress. Following her Academy Award–winning performance in *Reds*, she appeared in *Cocoon, Heartburn*, and *Addicted to Love*.

ROBERT WAGNER

✸

It's A Wrap!

✸

ROBERT WAGNER is a film and television star, perhaps best known for his roles in the *Pink Panther* movies and opposite Stefanie Powers in television's *Hart to Hart*.

BETTY WHITE

✸

Hopefully, Betty White will be remembered in the animal community as someone who had a passion for any creature with a leg on each corner. In the showbiz world, it may be said that she really tried. Ask anyone and they will tell you she was a most trying person.

✸

BETTY WHITE is an Emmy Award–winning actress, a Golden Girl, and an advocate for animal rights and pet care.

Game, Set, Match

ATHLETES AND SPORTS FIGURES

YOGI BERRA

∽∘∾

It's Over.

∽∘∾

YOGI BERRA is a former baseball star and coach. He was elected to the National Baseball Hall of Fame in 1972 and played for both the New York Yankees and the New York Mets.

BRIAN BOITANO

∽∘∾

Ice—blank page or canvas . . .
So many possibilities.

∽∘∾

BRIAN BOITANO is a world champion figure skater.

JIM BOUTON

✌o✍

Jim who?

✌o✍

JIM BOUTON is an all-star Major League baseball pitcher as well as a bestselling author. He also helped create and market Big League Chew, shredded bubble gum in a pouch.

BOB COUSY

✌o✍

He did his best when no one was watching.

✌o✍

BOB COUSY is a retired basketball star who was inducted into the Basketball Hall of Fame in 1970.

AL DAVIS

✌o✍

Based on team achievement, personal achievement, and contribution to the game, no one has had a more profound and lasting impact on the game of professional football than Al Davis.

The achievements of his team, the Raiders, are unmatched.

Davis's individual achievements are unequalled and because he dared to dream, he left a legacy of innovation that has changed the sport forever.

Al Davis loved his family, his team, his league and his country. He personified the words "loyalty," "friendship," and "passion" throughout his life.

∽○∾

AL DAVIS is a retired professional football player who was inducted into the Pro Football Hall of Fame in 1992.

DOMINIC DiMAGGIO

∽○∾

A guy who thrived on challenges large and small!

∽○∾

DOMINIC DIMAGGIO is a retired baseball player who played with the Boston Red Sox for eleven seasons. He is the brother of the late Joe DiMaggio, with whom he played in three All-Star Games.

ART DONOVAN

∽○∾

It's been a great ride; I wouldn't have missed it for the world.

∽○∾

ART DONOVAN is a retired professional football player who was inducted into the Pro Football Hall of Fame in 1968.

ANGELO DUNDEE

This was my corner of heaven! I had a lot of company and great champions! I was the person who always left a corner of the ring, but never stayed in the ring. The bell would ring, and I would get out of there. I was the guy with the short-sleeved white sweater with no name on the back.

ANGELO DUNDEE has trained fifteen world-champion boxers, including Muhammad Ali, Sugar Ray Leonard, George Foreman, and Sugar Ramos. He was inducted into the Boxing Hall of Fame in 1992.

JOE FRAZIER

I want to be remembered as being a good guy, one who always tried to help others in need.

SMOKIN' JOE FRAZIER is a boxing legend and former heavyweight champion of the world.

OTTO GRAHAM

❧∞❧

I want to be remembered as the son of musicians who taught me the rhythm and timing of music, which I carried into sports.

A lucky man, who often found himself in the right place at the right time, I have few regrets beyond losing a son to SIDS and the ability to savor life's precious memories due to Alzheimer's. Although Debussy's classic "Claire de Lune" has long been my favorite song, the modern lyrics of Dan Fogelberg put my achievements in perspective to those of my dad. I am a living legacy to the Leader of the Band.

❧∞❧

OTTO GRAHAM was a professional football player who was inducted into the Pro Football Hall of Fame in 1965. He died December 17, 2003.

DAN JANSEN

❧∞❧

After the 1988 Olympic Winter Olympic Games in Calgary, Canada, I thought I would always be remembered as the guy who fell after his sister Jane died of leukemia on the morning of his race.

Then after I won the gold medal at the 1994 Olympics in Lillehammer, Norway, I figured I would be remembered as the guy who didn't quit, never gave up on his dream, and finally succeeded in the end.

Those were both defining moments in my life, but they are not who I was. They only reflect who I was.

I would rather be remembered as someone who did my very

best in *everything* I did; someone who always gave 100%, not necessarily to be *the* best, but to be *my* best.

∽○∾

DAN JANSEN is an Olympic gold medalist and world record holder in speed skating.

BILLIE JEAN KING

∽○∾

Thank you and God Bless! I have had a great life, but I still have so much more to do!

∽○∾

BILLIE JEAN KING was a pioneer in women's sports. In 1967 she was named "Outstanding Female Athlete of the World" and in 1972 was named *Sports Illustrated*'s "Sportsperson of the Year," the first woman to be so honored.

BOBBY KNIGHT

∽○∾

When my time on earth is done
And I have breathed my last
I want they bury me upside down
So my critics can kiss my ass

BOBBY KNIGHT is one of the most successful college basketball coaches of all time. During his twenty-nine-year career coaching the Indiana University men's basketball team, he led the team to three national championships and 763 victories. He now coaches at Texas Tech University.

JERRY KOOSMAN

∽○∾

The first and last outs were easy—but all the ones in between gave me gray hair.

∽○∾

JERRY KOOSMAN is a retired pitcher who was the National League rookie pitcher of the year in 1968.

TOMMY LASORDA

∽○∾

Dodger Stadium was his address, but every ballpark was his home.

∽○∾

TOMMY LASORDA began his baseball career with the Brooklyn Dodgers in 1954 and went on to manage the Los Angeles Dodgers to two World Series titles and four National pennants. He was inducted into the Baseball Hall of Fame in 1997, the fourteenth honoree to be elected as a manager.

MEADOWLARK LEMON

❦

It's Just a Game; It's Not Life

I have played basketball for kings, presidents and even the Pope. Traveling over all the corners of the earth, you observe many things and many people, but in the end it's just a game; it's not life. You can experience a myriad of things and still not know the meaning of life.

Life is not measured by what you possess but by what possesses you. I have known most of the luxuries money can afford and the admiration that comes with fame.

The pleasure of signing autographs and meeting multitudes of smiling faces warms your heart. Yet, the greatest thrill, the greatest moment of my life, was when I was introduced to the architect of the whole universe and found he loved me for me, not what I could do.

I have been called the Clown Prince of Basketball, an ambassador of good cheer to the world, but to be a child of God is the highest honor anyone could have.

I hope today when you think of Meadowlark Lemon, you remember the most important thing, which is living for God is life and basketball is just a game.

❦

MEADOWLARK LEMON was part of the Harlem Globetrotters and was awarded the Basketball Hall of Fame Lifetime Achievement Award in 2000.

JACK NICKLAUS

✧

When I am gone, I'd like for them to say that in some small way I contributed to society. Most important, I'd like for them to say I was a good father, and that I certainly wasn't a stranger to my kids and grandkids. They knew me and I knew them.

✧

JACK NICKLAUS is a golfing legend. He holds the record for the most major tournament wins: twenty, including six Masters, five PGAs, four U.S. Opens, and three British Opens.

DEAN OLIVER

✧

When I'm gone, if someone will say about me, "He was a cowboy," that will be good enough for me.

✧

DEAN OLIVER is a world champion rodeo star and cowboy.

CAL RIPKEN

✧

From a personal standpoint, I would like to be remembered as a family man and someone who took on the positive attributes of and learned life lessons from wonderful, solid parents. Someone who did his best to show patience and understanding and valued the opinions and viewpoints of others.

Professionally, I would like to be remembered as someone who represented the game of baseball well. Someone who used the platform that baseball provided him to make a positive impact on kids. On the field, I would like baseball fans and players to remember me as a gamer. Somebody who came to play each and every day and faced the challenges of each day to the best of my ability.

✺

CAL RIPKEN is a former professional baseball player with the Baltimore Orioles. He is known as baseball's "Iron Man" for breaking Lou Gehrig's consecutive games streak in 1995; Ripken played 2,632 consecutive games from the start of his career with the Orioles in 1982 until his retirement in 1998.

PHIL RIZZUTO

✺

I would like to be remembered as a person who brought much happiness to people through the wonderful game of baseball while having an angel on my shoulder. I was so lucky it was unbelievable!

✺

PHIL RIZZUTO was a part of the Yankee dynasty, helping the team win seven of nine World Series during his tenure. He was inducted into the Baseball Hall of Fame in 1994.

DON SHULA

❦

A man of faith, a family man, and a man that rose to the top of his profession. Raised a Catholic, a graduate of John Carroll University, and a daily communicant whenever possible. Married with five children and now an extended family that includes eight children and fourteen grandchildren.

Being inducted into the NFL Hall of Fame in 1997 was the ultimate recognition of my career in the NFL, and being presented for induction by my two sons Dave and Mike in front of so many friends and family made the day all the more memorable.

With the opportunity also comes the responsibility to attempt to give something back. This can be done by trying to set the right example whenever possible and to support the many worthwhile charitable organizations that need all the help we can give.

The peace of mind we search for will come when we feel we've done all that we can do with the opportunities God gave us.

❦

DON SHULA is a retired professional football coach who holds the NFL record for most games won in a career. He was inducted into the Pro Football Hall of Fame in 1997.

Out

of

Print

AUTHORS AND WRITERS

✥

MAYA ANGELOU

୧୦ଠ୦

Get a hot roasted chicken, a good loaf of French bread and a cold bottle of chardonnay, eat it all and enjoy and remember me when I'm gone.

୧୦ଠ୦

MAYA ANGELOU is a poet, author, playwright, and civil rights activist. She is the author of several bestselling books, including *I Know Why the Caged Bird Sings*, and is a professor of American studies at Wake Forest University.

CARL SFERRAZZA ANTHONY

୧୦ଠ୦

He always found that he enjoyed life more when he engaged others. When he spoke with people, he never feared hearing of their problems. He enjoyed helping others to see the good in their lives; doing so also warded off his sense of alienation. A definitive truth he discovered was that everyone usually had the same fears at one point or another; this always dissipated his own fears. He always tried to remind himself, and then others, that he and they were no worse or no better, intrinsically, than any other person. He found this especially important in dealing with the powerful figures he encountered, whether meeting those who were alive, or writing about those who were not. He always sought to discover their elemental humanity—whether they be attributes or deficiencies. When others feared death and what might or might not follow it, he always reminded them that every human, regardless of status, passes through the exact same door and encounters the same experience. He tried to remember this himself, too.

CARL SFERRAZZA ANTHONY is the author of several books on American presidents and their families.

PIERS ANTHONY

Piers Anthony, maverick, liberal, agnostic, independent, vegetarian, health nut. No belief in the supernatural, yet made his living from fantasy. Wrote readable books, made readers smile, learn, and think; helped some to learn to read, write, publish, and live. Longed to understand man and the universe, and to leave the world marginally better than he found it. Tried to do the decent thing.

PIERS ANTHONY is the author of more than one hundred science-fiction novels and is the creator of the Xanth fantasy series.

70

JENNIFER BLAKE

❦

An optimist by nature, she wrote about love and "happily ever after" because she lived them, and chose always to portray the higher aspects of human nature with emphasis on ideals and extreme notions of honor. Her purpose as she saw it, however, was not to inform or instruct but to bring the joy of love and laughter into the lives of her readers. The sheer joy of being alive was a recurrent theme, running like a thread of gold through the fabric of her work.

❦

JENNIFER BLAKE is a bestselling and award-winning romance novelist.

JACK CANFIELD

❦

He helped heal the world . . . one story at a time.

❦

JACK CANFIELD is a bestselling author and the co-creator and founder of the *Chicken Soup for the Soul* book series.

JACKIE COLLINS

❧∞❧

She gave a great many people a great deal of pleasure.

❧∞❧

JACKIE COLLINS is a bestselling and award-winning author whose books have sold more than 300 million copies worldwide. She is the author of more than twenty *New York Times* bestsellers.

CLIVE CUSSLER

❧∞❧

It was a great party while it lasted.
I trust it will continue elsewhere.

❧∞❧

CLIVE CUSSLER is a bestselling author, with nearly one million copies of his Dirk Pitt novels in circulation worldwide.

JANET DAILEY

❧∞❧

To my husband Bill, who—if there was a secret to my success, it was his support, guidance and sound business sense—once told me, "Don't worry about the money. If the book you've written is good, it will come. You won't be able to stop it." As usual, he was absolutely right.

To be honest, my career always took second place to my family and friends. Without them, all the success I might have achieved would have meant absolutely nothing.

❧

JANET DAILEY is a bestselling novelist and a pioneer in the genre of romance novels. Her books have sold more than 300 million copies worldwide.

FANNIE FLAGG

❧

Does this mean the book tour is over?

❧

FANNIE FLAGG is a bestselling novelist. Her numerous books include *Fried Green Tomatoes at the Whistle Stop Café*, which was adapted into a major motion picture.

URI GELLER

❧

I hope that by remembering my name you will be positive, you will be optimistic, you will stay hopeful, believing in yourself and having faith. From the other side I send you health, happiness and peace of mind.

❦

ANDREW GREELEY

❦

When Father Andrew Greeley heard that a University of Chicago sociologist said that he was nothing but a loud-mouthed Irish priest, he replied, "Put that on my tombstone."

He was a Cub fan and a junkyard dog Democrat. However, he did not deny the possibility that some Republicans could find salvation. In fact, he often prayed for their salvation. He tried to make his own the epitaph of Hilaire Belloc:

> *May it be said*
> *When I am dead*
> *His sins were scarlet*
> *His books were read.*

❦

ARTHUR HAILEY

A Last Request

Over my helpless, mute remains
Please do not play barbaric games,
Nor cast a superstitious nod
Toward some non-existent god.
Instead, respect my intellect,
Which made me, thoughtfully, reject
Man's wishful, vain, deceiving scrimmage—
Creating gods in his own image.

I've relished life; on earth found "heaven,"
Known love and joy, received and given.
I do not need Elysian vales—
The stuff of flimsy fairy tales!
I'd much prefer that you, my friend,
Conclude my story with "The End."

ARTHUR HAILEY is a bestselling novelist whose books, including *Airport* and *Hotel*, have sold more than 170 million copies worldwide in forty languages.

EARL HAMNER

❦

I put my hometown on the map. I wish that I could take it off.*

*Local people complain because of increased traffic, inquisitive tourists, and disruption of their previously tranquil way of life.

❦

EARL HAMNER is a novelist and television writer. He created and produced the Emmy Award–winning programs *The Waltons* and *Falcon Crest*. His most recent book is *Goodnight, John Boy*.

EVAN HUNTER

❦

He wrote like an angel.

❦

EVAN HUNTER is a bestselling novelist who has written more than fifty novels and screenplays. He also writes under the pseudonym Ed McBain.

JOHN IRVING

❧

Destiny is not imaginable, except in dreams or to those in love.

—excerpted from *The Fourth Hand* by John Irving

❧

JOHN IRVING is a bestselling novelist whose novels have been translated into more than thirty languages worldwide. He won an Academy Award for writing the screenplay for the movie based on his novel *The Cider House Rules*.

JOHN JAKES

❧

He was a good storyteller, and when he told stories of the American past, he was at his best.

❧

JOHN JAKES is a *New York Times* bestselling novelist who specializes in historical fiction. His latest work is *Charleston*.

ERICA JONG

Here lies
Erica Mann Jong
poet and novelist

Since flesh can't stay,
we pass the words along.

ERICA JONG is the author of eight novels as well as a variety of other books of nonfiction and poetry. Many of her novels, including *Fear of Flying*, have been national bestsellers.

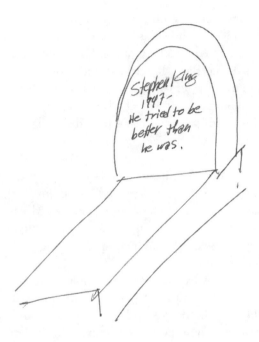

He tried to be better than he was.

STEPHEN KING is one of the world's foremost novelists.

❧

The Hyper Life: Obituary of a Deep Cover Agent

I was born at age nineteen on the day that I was supposed to die. My intended killer's name was Heywood; we were both military cops assigned to the 380th Combat Defense Squadron at Plattsburgh Air Force Base. It was a stupid little argument over a $3 hat. I don't even remember what I said, but before I took my next breath, Heywood smacked me full in the face, drew his .45-caliber semi-automatic and pulled the trigger.

I can still hear that hollow *click*.

The gun had misfired.

The gun muzzle still exists in my mind's eye as if it had a will of its own, huge and black in Heywood's hand, just inches from the middle of my chest. Heywood's eyes glazed white, the size of saucers with pinpoint pupils going from the gun to me, to the gun again. Astonished. Uncomprehending.

Heywood was arrested.

The gun was tested by experts. It worked fine; it fired every time. The bullet's casing had been perforated perfectly dead center; it *should* have fired. No technical reason could be given for this anomaly. The expert told me that it's the kind of thing that just happens once every 10 million rounds or so. A .45-caliber bullet would have blown me in half.

On that day, I learned the wisdom of an old Arab saying: "Any day is a perfect day to die." On that day, I came out of the dark fog of a birth canal that for most people endures to the grave. On that day, I was born with a ravenous hunger to *experience* everything and anything as quickly as I could, always aware that *this* day might be that perfect day.

From that day on, I lived in the golden glow of adventure, heightened senses, hyper experiences pumped with an incessant flow of adrenaline. What better passport for a poor kid from the South Bronx to the hyper life than a career as a deep cover agent, assuming fantasy identities, traveling from one alien world to the next. From Chinese heroin dealers in the Golden Triangle during the Vietnam War to South American cocaine cartels during the Cocoa Revolution in Bolivia.

I became Miguel Garcia, Mike Pagano, Mohamed Kahn, Luis Lopez and dozens of others, adopting and absorbing entire lives and personalities; whatever was needed to seduce, join and destroy to get the job done. I forgot who I was at birth, but never forgot who I would be at death. I won total acceptance, trust and even devotion, and then betrayed that trust, leaving in my wake thousands of bodies spending thousands of lifetimes in cages—and death much death. There were more guns that didn't fire and many bullets that missed. More luck than fate is supposed to allow; more third, fourth and fifth chances than any mortal has a right to expect.

And the men in suits said that it was all good.

And I wanted badly to believe them.

But I learned that the hyper life, the deep cover life, came with great pain and self-doubt. When my twenty-seven-year-old son, Keith Richard Levine, a New York City cop, took a bullet in his heart while trying to stop a robbery, I was convinced that on some level in the cosmos, my baby boy had been selected to take the bullet—all the bullets—that had failed to kill his father.

For a long time I wished Heywood's bullet had fired.

And I really began to wonder about the "why."

Then I met my wife, Laura. We made love and danced the Mambo, and I had my answer.

MICHAEL LEVINE is a *New York Times* bestselling author as well as an acclaimed public speaker, retired federal agent, and host of *The Expert Witness* radio program. His books include *Deep Cover, Fight Back,* and *The Big White Lie.*

JOHN NANCE

How would I like to be remembered?

How about with a great single-malt scotch on a snowy evening by a roaring fire, speaking through the pages of one of my books?

Actually, that's the very reason I wanted to become an author—to outlive myself on the shelves of libraries and in the memories of satisfied readers who spent many hours letting me use the medium of print to whisper in their ear, maybe even teaching them a few things I'd discovered.

JOHN NANCE is an internationally recognized air safety analyst and advocate. He is the aviation analyst for *ABC World News* and *Good Morning America* and the bestselling author of *Skyhook*, *Blackout*, and *Pandora's Clock*.

TIM O'BRIEN

He was a boy, and then a man, hungry for love. His appetite was huge. He smiled and nodded and laughed and cried for love, performed magic for love, drank for love, smoked for love, went to war for love, wrote his books for love, did good things and bad things—grand things and ugly things—only for love.

TIM O'BRIEN is an award-winning author and the recipient of the 1979 National Book Award for fiction for his work *Going After Cacciato*. He is the author of *July, July*; *If I Die in a Combat Zone*; *Nuclear Age*; and *The Things They Carried*, a Pulitzer Prize finalist.

FREDERIK POHL

༺⊶༻

He did the best he could, mostly.

༺⊶༻

FREDERIK POHL is a science-fiction writer and the editor of several science-fiction anthologies. His works include *The Far Shore of Time*, *Tales from the Planet Earth*, and *O Pioneer!*

HERMAN RAUCHER

༺⊶༻

Here Lies Herman Raucher—
One of the finest writers who ever died.

༺⊶༻

HERMAN RAUCHER is an author. He wrote *Summer of '42* and its screenplay, which was nominated for four Academy Awards in 1971.

LEON URIS

My deepest sorrow is for Larry King
The great interviewer of our times
Whose collection is tragically incomplete
Because he never interviewed me.

LEON URIS was a bestselling novelist, perhaps best known for his 1958 novel, *Exodus*. He passed away on June 21, 2003.

Back to the Drawing Board

CARTOONISTS AND ARTISTS

SCOTT ADAMS

∽o∾

I took it with me.

∽o∾

SCOTT ADAMS is the creator of the award-winning comic strip *Dilbert* and the author of several bestselling books.

JIM DAVIS

∽o∾

I would like to be remembered as someone who was extremely old.

∽o∾

JIM DAVIS is the Emmy Award–winning creator of the comic strip *Garfield*, which is syndicated in more than 2,600 newspapers worldwide.

J. C. DUFFY

J. C. DUFFY is the creator of the comic strip *The Fusco Brothers*, as well as the author of several books.

ROB HARRELL

"Ba - Dump - Bump."

ROB HARRELL is a cartoonist whose drawings have appeared in a wide variety of newspapers and magazines.

SANDY HUFFAKER

❦

The last KNOWN picture of Sandy Huffaker (on the left).

❦

SANDY HUFFAKER is a political cartoonist who has been nominated for a Pulitzer Prize.

LARRY KATZMAN

"This isn't Hollywood."

LARRY KATZMAN is a nationally syndicated cartoonist.

BIL KEANE

∽∘∾

Did you ever realize that the little dash between the two dates on your gravestone (birth and death) will represent your entire lifetime?

I pray that squeezed into that dash on my stone are moments of pleasure, laughter, insight, and precious family memories brought to my readers through the years.

If so, I will be happy to have dashed for so many decades before running out of breath.

∽∘∾

BIL KEANE is the creator of the award-winning comic strip *The Family Circus,* as well as the author of several books.

HANK KETCHAM

HANK KETCHAM was the award-winning creator of the comic strip *Dennis the Menace*, which was based on his own son. He passed away on June 1, 2001.

DICK LOCHER

ALL POINTS BULLETIN to the SUPREME CHIEF.

Be on the lookout for DICK TRACY artist and Pulitzer Prize winning editorial cartoonist, DICK LOCHER. He is armed with ideas and is considered irreverent and irascible. He impaled injustice with his wit and shot down foes with his pen and ink. This Dragon slayer has now run out of time. DICK LOCHER has met his final deadline.

That's a big 10 – 4, Sir.

© TRIBUNE MEDIA SERVICES

DICK LOCHER is a Pulitzer Prize–winning editorial cartoonist for the *Chicago Tribune* and illustrator of the *Dick Tracy* cartoon strip.

GARY MARKSTEIN

GARY MARKSTEIN is a nationally syndicated editorial cartoonist for the *Milwaukee Journal Sentinel.*

A very personal eulogy

TIM MENEES draws editorial cartoons for the *Pittsburgh Post-Gazette*. He has no intention of delivering this anytime soon and hopes everyone will understand.

STEVE MOORE is the creator of the comic strip *In the Bleachers* as well as the author of several books.

LENNIE PETERSON

∽o∾

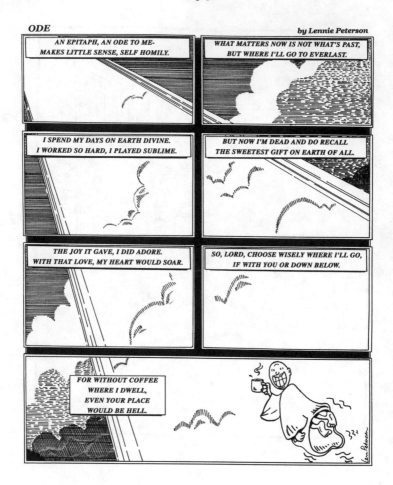

∽o∾

LENNIE PETERSON is the internationally syndicated creator of the comic strip *The Big Picture*, which is based on his own life.

JIM PHILLIPS is a nationally syndicated political cartoonist for the *Toronto Sun*.

WAYNE STAYSKAL

WAYNE STAYSKAL is an editorial cartoonist for the *Tampa Tribune*.

DANA SUMMERS is a political cartoonist for the *Orlando Sentinel*.

FINISHING TOUCH

CORKY TRINIDAD is an editorial cartoonist for the *Honolulu Star-Bulletin*.

MORT WALKER

✂⌘✂

I'D LIKE TO BE REMEMBERED AS A WORLD LEADER IN THE ARTS, A GREAT WRITER, A WAR VETERAN, A PATRIOT, A WONDERFUL HUSBAND AND FATHER, A FOUNDER OF A MARVELOUS MUSEUM AND A BELOVED HUMORIST.

BUT I'LL PROBABLY BE REMEMBERED AS "WHAT'S-HIS-NAME" WHO WAS PAID MORE THAN HIS DOODLES WERE WORTH.

©K.F.S.

✂⌘✂

MORT WALKER is an award-winning cartoonist and creator of the comic strips *Beetle Bailey* and *Hi & Lois*.

Getting the Last Laugh

COMEDIANS AND COMEDIENNES

BERNIE ALLEN

We don't stop laughing because we grow old. We grow old because we stop laughing.

BERNIE ALLEN has been in the business of making people laugh since Frank Sinatra helped him get his start over sixty years ago. He now devotes a great deal of his time to organizing charity events to help the homeless.

DAVID BRENNER

My epitaph, or, rather, epitaphs, because I am going to have a Side A and Side B on my stone (why not, it's the same price, right?) will be "Here lies David Brenner, born so and so, died so and so. He lived; he died, but man, did he live!" The flip side will read "Here lies David Brenner, born so and so, died so and so. If this is supposed to be funny, I don't get it."

DAVID BRENNER is a popular stand-up and television comedian. His political humor has landed him four HBO specials and guest appearances on many talk shows, including *The Tonight Show* and *Late Night with David Letterman*. He has also written several bestselling books.

RED BUTTONS

❦

I never got a dinner and now I don't need one.

❦

RED BUTTONS is an award-winning comedian and actor. He has acted on Broadway, starred in his own television show, *The Red Buttons Show*, and appeared in many movies, including *Sayonara*, for which he won both an Academy Award and a Golden Globe Award. His famous "Never Got a Dinner" routine was a favorite of the Dean Martin Celebrity Roasts.

SID CAESAR

❦

At least I made some people laugh!

❦

SID CAESAR is a comedic actor who got his start during World War II, performing his comedy routine in a revue put on by the United States Coast Guard. He went on to star in several revue-style television shows, *Admiral Broadway Review*, and *Your Show of Shows*. He has also enjoyed numerous film credits, including his roles in such popular movies as *Silent Movie* and *Grease*.

GEORGE CARLIN

✑✎

He wasn't a schmuck.

✑✎

GEORGE CARLIN is a Grammy Award–winning actor and comedian. The first host of *Saturday Night Live* in 1975, his most famous routine, "Seven Words You Can't Say on Television," brought him his most controversial fame. He has published three books, including most recently *Napalm & Silly Putty*.

JACK CARTER

✑✎

I told you I was sick! What's so funny? This is not funny. This is my last laugh.

Here lies Jack Carter, a famous comedian and a wonderful human being--Imagine, burying three guys in one plot!

Don't just stand there! Laugh!

✑✎

JACK CARTER got his start in comedy through his work in nightclubs. Since then, he has hosted a number of television variety shows, including *Cavalcade of Stars* and *Stage Show*. He has also guest starred on dozens of sitcoms and in the films *The Amazing Dobermans* and *The Funny Farm*.

MARGARET CHO

≈

I told you I was sick. How many times did I say it? I wasn't feeling well, I was under the weather, I wasn't getting better, just worse. You didn't listen to me. You told me to buck up, snap out of it, take some aspirin and call me in the morning. Well, I can't now because I'm dead. You idiot. All you care about is you and since my illness didn't include *you* I guess it didn't even exist. You're so vain. You probably think this eulogy is about you. But it isn't. Okay, maybe just a little bit. Because now that I am dead, I can tell you how stupid I think you are. And the fact that even though I pretended that I was your friend, I actually despised you. Yes, *you*! Isn't that a laugh? In fact, I fell in love with hating you. I would go out of my way to see you and be with you to hear you say things that I hated so that I could say them over and over to myself and feel superior and so glad that I wasn't you. I am going to miss that. Really and truly. The one thing I will miss on this earth is hating your guts. Which is probably what killed me. I put so much of my energy into hating you that I didn't have any left over to fight disease. So, you killed me. I hope you feel bad. But that probably won't happen. Because since you only think about you, and this is marginally about me, I know you will forget it as soon as you hear it. I know you are not even listening right now because you are thinking about what you are going to have for lunch. Basically, all I want you to remember is this. *F—— you!* I hope I see you soon.

≈

MARGARET CHO is an award-winning comedienne who has appeared in a dozen films and performed before sold-out audiences nationwide. She is the author of *I'm the One That I Want*. The movie version of her latest performance, *The Notorious C.H.O. at Carnegie Hall*, was released in 2002 to rave reviews.

BILL DANA

❦

While the specifics of the after-life elude us, there are some very pleasant aspects of death that make it something worth looking forward to. Here are the first few that leap to mind:

1. You can miss all the appointments you want, and no one will be mad at you for being late.
2. No matter how much you partied the night before, you won't wake up with a hangover.
3. It becomes socially acceptable for you to forget people's birthdays.
4. If you are overdue paying back a loan shark, he may still break your legs . . . but so what?
5. For those of you who have always wanted to be written up in the newspaper, but never did anything that warranted it—this ought to do it.
6. The importance of health food is greatly reduced.
7. The lies people tell about you will be in your favor.

But what happens after we die? You can make your own guess about what lies in the Great Beyond. Be as creative as you like and don't feel constrained by conventional conjecture. The important thing is that your after-life scenario entertains you. And, for all you know, you might be right.

❦

BILL DANA is a comedian, writer, and performer. He was a contributing writer to *The Steve Allen Show* in the 1950s and 1960s. He is perhaps best known for his portrayals of José Jimenez, the easily confused, heavily accented character he developed and played on several television programs and variety shows in the 1960s.

PHYLLIS DILLER

❧

I would like to be remembered for being kind and un-pushy.

❧

PHYLLIS DILLER is a female pioneer in the field of comedy. She is known for her over-the-top wigs, outfits, and unique laugh. She has also appeared in films and has devoted her time to various philanthropic activities such as cancer research.

ARTE JOHNSON

❧

I seem to have run out of tomorrows.

❧

ARTE JOHNSON is an Emmy Award–winning comedian who is perhaps best known for his performances on *Rowan and Martin's Laugh-In*, including his portrayal of the unforgettable German soldier with the trademark line, "Verrrrry interesting."

DENIS LEARY

❧

The jig is up.

❧

DENIS LEARY is a comedian, actor, director, producer, and writer known for his dry and acerbic style. He got his comedic break in Edinburgh where he won the Critic's Award at the Edinburgh International Arts Festival for his "No Cure for Cancer" routine. Since then, he has starred in a multitude of films, including *National Lampoon's Loaded Weapon* and *The Ref*.

HOWIE MANDEL

౿ం౾

Is it me or did it just get dark in here?

౿ం౾

HOWIE MANDEL is a comedian who has performed in nightclubs and on film and television. He found great success in television, starring in the award-winning series *St. Elsewhere* and hosting his own talk show, *The Howie Mandel Show*, as well as creating, producing, and writing for the successful children's animated series *Bobby's World*. He has also created several educational computer games for children.

MARILYN MICHAELS

౿ం౾

As a comedienne, I spent my life as a thousand other people but unfortunately I get to die as myself! So, here I am on my back for the final time, and it ain't even fun. And I'm wondering what some of those people whose voices and faces that I gave new life to would say about my demise.

Barbra: I never crossed my eyes like that. She deserves this, and I'd like to rain on her parade!

Dr. Ruth: I told her be more sexual, life is so short, not as short as me, but short! Have fun, go to the ball. After all, who knows more about balls than I do!

Elizabeth Taylor: After calling Richard, Hamlet and me "piglet," I was *never* fat, I was only bloated. Very, very bloated . . .

Julie Andrews: I never sang flat, that was an egregious remark.

Joan Rivers: Oh sure, before she had that nose job, ugh, she had to blindfold her vibrator!

Greta Garbo: I wanted to be alone, but this is ridiculous.

Liza: She lied about me; I never took that much Valium. Did I just get married again? To whom?

Roseanne: She always made fun of my weight; finally, a diet that works!

Zsa Zsa: I never liked cold and damp and neither did she. We should have taken our furs.

∽⚬∾

MARILYN MICHAELS is a multitalented performer who is best known for her impersonations and guest appearances on television shows such as *The Tonight Show*. She is also an actress and a singer.

PAULA POUNDSTONE

❦

A recycler. She raised wonderful children. When all was tallied, without cooking the books, the world was no worse off for having had her around.

❦

PAULA POUNDSTONE is a comedienne who performs a conversation-style stand-up routine in her characteristic suit jacket and tie. She hosted a comedy series on HBO and ABC and won an Emmy Award for her work on the PBS special *Life and Times*.

MARK RUSSELL

❦

Born—Buffalo, NY
Died—Buffalo, NY
(Several Times)

❦

MARK RUSSELL is a political humorist who complements his comedic act with his own piano riffs. Dubbed "Washington's Other Monument," his PBS comedy special is in its twenty-seventh season. He is also a commentator on CNN's *Inside Politics Weekend* and a syndicated columnist.

SOUPY SALES

∽◦∾

Here lies the body of Soupy Sales.
If not, call James Rabe—funeral at once!

∽◦∾

SOUPY SALES is a comedic actor and humorist. His work has ranged from radio shows to nightclub stand-up to television programs. He is known for his off-the-wall humor and famous pie-throwing gag.

Final Audit

ENTREPRENEURS AND PEOPLE IN BUSINESS

WALLY AMOS

❧❀❧

He lived his Statement of Purpose, helping people feel good about themselves. He did it by serving others and making good chocolate chip cookies.

❧❀❧

WALLY "FAMOUS" AMOS is the father of the gourmet cookie industry. He is also an inspirational speaker and a devoted sponsor of literacy causes.

ROCKY AOKI

❧❀❧

I have been blessed to live a life full of excitement and happiness. I have always done what I want. And for some odd reason I have been fortunate doing it. The gods have been watching me. My advice to all of you is to challenge yourself till your last second of life and retire with me in heaven.

❧❀❧

ROCKY AOKI is the founder of the Benihana chain of Japanese restaurants. Combining dining with entertainment, skilled Japanese chefs prepare meals on a tableside grill to the amazement of dining patrons at his establishments.

TOVA BORGNINE

༒

God made man.
Tova made man notice women.
She made women feel beautiful.
Passion was her beauty and beauty was her passion.
Tova was here but now she's gone. She leaves her scent to
   carry on.
Remember to blend your eye shadow
And never go to bed with your makeup on.
An eye for beauty, a nose for fragrance and two arms to
   embrace life warmly.
Now I can finally say it's the bergamot.
She lived for beauty, for the joy of sharing it.

༒

TOVA BORGNINE is a pioneer in the women's fragrance and beauty industry. She is the host of the highly popular QVC program *Beauty by Tova*, and runs her own salon, Mind, Body, Spirit, in Beverly Hills.

NORMAN BROKAW

༒

Dedication. Passion. Loyalty. These are the qualities that stayed with me throughout my career, and served me well during my journey from the mail room to the board room and at home in the family room.

These are the qualities I tried to impart to the young agent trainees as they set out on their own careers in the entertainment industry. For the deals will come and go, and come and go again, but it is the people we touch and the people who touch us that make everything worthwhile.

‌❧

NORMAN R. BROKAW is the chairman of the William Morris Agency in New York City, which represents and promotes a multitude of famous actors, athletes, authors, and musicians.

JENNY CRAIG

❧

I saw it all
I did it all
I loved it all
I bought it all
The rest I gave away
Goodbye!

❧

JENNY CRAIG is the CEO and founder of the Jenny Craig weight loss system. Her company has helped millions worldwide achieve their weight loss goals.

MICHAEL EISNER

❦

All things considered, Michael D. Eisner would rather now be reading this than having written it.

❦

MICHAEL D. EISNER is chairman and CEO of the Walt Disney Company.

STEVE FORBES

❦

The income tax is now flat—but, alas, so am I.

❦

STEVE FORBES is CEO and editor in chief of *Forbes* magazine.

TOMMY HILFIGER

❦

An all-American classic designer who brought class to the masses.

❦

TOMMY HILFIGER is a fashion designer who is perhaps best known for his touching renditions of Americana clothing, particularly through the use of his distinctive red, white, and blue color scheme.

CALVIN KLEIN

❦

Calvin Klein by Eternity

❦

CALVIN KLEIN is one of the most influential fashion designers of the twenty-first century. In addition to a full line of clothing for men, women, and children, he also produces beauty and cosmetic products.

JACK LaLANNE

❦

What I would like to be remembered for is, not especially for the guy who developed the leg extension, the wall-pulley weight-selector machines, or swam from Alcatraz handcuffed and shackled, but somebody who practiced what he preached and had one thing on his mind: not making a lot of money, but trying to help people to a better way of life.

So help yourself to a better way of life through exercise, proper nutrition, and positive thinking. Anything in this life is possible, if you make it happen. So make it happen!

❦

JACK LALANNE is a fitness and health guru who, for more than twenty years, was the host of *The Jack LaLanne Show*, a fitness and exercise program designed for homemakers. He writes and lectures widely on the importance of diet and exercise for all people.

BILL McCARTNEY

❧

The Bible teaches that if we have all knowledge, understand all mysteries, possess complete faith—the kind that will move mountains, give all our goods to the poor, and offer our bodies to be burned for a great cause, but have not love, our lives count for nothing. Please remember me as a man whose heart was selfish and prideful, yet Jesus Christ came into this heart and taught it to love. I am learning to love others unconditionally as God's Holy Spirit takes dominion in my heart. I am growing a little each day. This love never fails.

❧

BILL McCARTNEY is the founder of Promise Keepers, an organization dedicated to igniting and uniting men to be passionate followers of Jesus Christ.

FRANK PERDUE

❧

Frank Perdue will probably best be remembered in years to come as the tough man who made tender chickens based on the advertising campaign he launched in the early 1970s that took the country by storm and made marketing history with the first successful branding of a commodity product.

Despite his success and fame, Frank Perdue remained a farm boy. He lived a simple life, and, when not checking up on the business, was often at the minor-league baseball park named after his father, Arthur Perdue, following the hometown team. Frank never moved from his native Salisbury, and the community benefited from his generosity. Frank also practiced a quiet philanthropy, responding to the needs in the communities where his associates work, often with gestures known only to Frank and the grateful recipients.

Frank Perdue's success was derived first from a solid foundation of values and attitudes that came from his father, and second from a vast superstructure of drive and ability to grow, combined with world-class ability to see, shape and create opportunity where others saw none, and to build that opportunity into success. His success, in the end, is indeed a fruit of labor, thought and *genius*.

FRANK PERDUE is the founder of the Perdue Chicken Company.

DONALD TRUMP

A man of great vision, who fulfilled many of his dreams, loved his family and was loyal to his friends.

DONALD TRUMP is the chairman and CEO of Trump Hotels and Casino Resorts.

The Ink

Has Run

Dry

JOURNALISTS AND REPORTERS

WALTER ANDERSON

❧

Behold my magic. I can cast a thought a thousand miles, through storm and stone, even beyond time. Long after my flesh has withered and my bones have crumbled to dust, the very best of me—my ideas, my dreams—can live, can burn with undiminished fire and passion. All because I have a gift, a power, and I am not alone. You share my miracle: You cannot touch me, but I am here; you cannot see me, but I am real. At this very moment, I am alive in your mind. We call this miracle *language*.

❧

WALTER ANDERSON is the chairman and CEO of *Parade* magazine. In 1998 he published *The Confidence Course: Seven Steps to Self-Fulfillment*, a book offering readers advice on how to gain confidence and succeed in life. He is also an advocate for literacy causes.

DAVE BARRY

❧

Dave's not here.

❧

DAVE BARRY is a nationally and internationally syndicated columnist and humorist. He won a Pulitzer Prize for commentary in 1988.

MARILYN BECK

✼

Remember me not for any professional achievements, but for the love—and a bit of wisdom perhaps—I bestowed on my children and grandchildren. As a wise man once said, buildings crumble, empires fall—love is the only thing that is eternal as it is passed from one generation to another.

✼

MARILYN BECK is an award-winning syndicated columnist. Her extensive research reports on the entertainment industry cover the action on the set, behind-the-scenes, and in the industry's boardrooms.

DAVID BRINKLEY

✼

I always tried to tell the truth.

✼

DAVID BRINKLEY was a multiple Emmy and George Foster Peabody Award–winning newsman who developed and modernized the medium of broadcast journalism. Nicknamed "the elder statesman of broadcast journalism," he was a commentator and co-anchor for *The Huntley-Brinkley Report*, *NBC Nightly News*, *This Week with David Brinkley*, and ABC's *World News Tonight*. He passed away on June 12, 2003.

JOYCE BROTHERS

✌∽

She tried her very best to be helpful to people.

✌∽

DR. JOYCE BROTHERS writes a daily syndicated popular psychology newspaper column. She makes numerous guest appearances as herself in movies and on television.

HELEN GURLEY BROWN

✌∽

What I'd like to be remembered for is helping women, however few or many, have better lives in terms of realizing potential sexually, professionally, personally. Maybe they were mouseburgers like me who didn't think they had what it took to be good in those areas but gradually, just by doing the best they could every day if not every minute, their efforts paid off and they were in a position to help other women do the same thing. Through the years at airports, restaurants, bus-stop benches, grocery stores, women have introduced themselves and told me I'd helped them with a book or magazine; they didn't need to do that if they weren't sincere. Okay, having helped any at all, however much or little, is what I want to be remembered for.

✌∽

HELEN GURLEY BROWN is the former editor in chief of *Cosmopolitan* magazine. Her books, most notably *Sex and the Single Girl*, spoke to young women of the sixties about sexual freedom and revolution.

∽○∽

As the lone woman (and often lone liberal) appearing regularly on *The McLaughlin Group*, a testosterone-driven debate show, a week rarely goes by without me saying—well, screaming—Let me finish! My goal is to finish a sentence without being interrupted. As soon as I start speaking, I can see my fellow panelists begin to levitate, ready to pounce while I'm still in mid-thought. An apt epitaph for me would be "Let Me Finish." But that got me thinking. Can life be tidily wrapped up and turned in like a sound bite, or an opinion column? Death is an end point and the orderly, Germanic side of me would like everything in order, all writing projects completed and deadlines met. But life is never finished. There is always something left undone that beckons us. So when I leave this earth, I expect I'll be protesting, "Let Me Finish," and I'll be grateful that I didn't take life for granted, and always wanted more.

∽○∽

ELEANOR CLIFT is a contributing editor for *Newsweek* magazine. She is a regular commentator on the nationally syndicated news program *The McLaughlin Group*, and has appeared as herself in a variety of television programs and feature films.

CATHERINE CRIER

∽○∽

The epitaph that I believe sums up my more noble behavior in life would read "Courage to Risk, Freedom to Fail." This has been my motto for years and has spurred me to undertake challenges that have truly shaped my life. On the other hand, my friends in law school awarded me a different exit line. Impatient with long-winded persons or meetings filled with trivial matters, I would frequently excuse myself by saying, "If this is essentially it, I'm gone!" This is probably the better choice!

∽o∾

CATHERINE CRIER is the host of *Catherine Crier Live*, a daily television program that addresses the legal perspective of the day's "front page" story. An Emmy Award–winning journalist, she was the youngest state judge elected in Texas, in 1984.

PHIL DONAHUE

∽o∾

Is the caller there?

∽o∾

PHIL DONAHUE began his career as a talk-show host in 1967. His Emmy Award–winning show *Donahue* helped establish the genre of the daytime talk show. Over the years, he has interviewed hundreds of celebrities, political leaders, athletes, and authors.

HUGH DOWNS

∞

A lucky and grateful human, who hopes he is remembered as a man of some integrity.

∞

HUGH DOWNS is a multiple Emmy Award–winning broadcaster and journalist. He is the former co-anchor of ABC's *20/20* and the author of ten books. During his sixty-four-year career in radio and television, he also hosted *Today* and helped launch *The Tonight Show*.

DOMINICK DUNNE

∞

I knew Dominick Dunne. I interviewed him on several occasions when he had a new book out, or when he covered a famous murder trial. I always found him to be remarkably forthcoming when he discussed his life. He had experienced failure and he had experienced fame. He had known heartbreak. His daughter had been murdered. One of his sons was estranged from him. His writing was praised and damned. Important people liked him. Important people despised him. Sometimes he was in the news: a disgraced former congressman sued him for slander; an assassinated president's nephew accused him of being responsible for the indictment of his cousin for murder. His name was in the columns. He appeared on television talk shows. He was welcomed by the captains at fashionable restaurants. He knew everybody. He went everywhere. He was a lonely man, but he felt lucky. He had a son he loved who was a great comfort to him. He had a granddaughter he worshiped. His last words as he lay dying were a sort of prayer. "Thank you for my life," he said.

DOMINICK DUNNE is an investigative journalist who has covered the most influential and high-profile murder trials of our time. He is a *Vanity Fair* columnist and the author of several bestselling books, including *The Two Mrs. Grenvilles, People Like Us*, and *An Inconvenient Woman*.

BOB GUCCIONE

Remember me when I'm gone
If I've touched you in any way
Remember though I'm travelin' on
We're sure to meet again one day.

BOB GUCCIONE is the publisher of *Penthouse* magazine.

HUGH HEFNER

୬୦ல

I'd like to be remembered as someone who played some part in changing our hurtful and hypocritical views on sex—and had a lot of fun doing it.

୬୦ல

HUGH HEFNER is the publisher of *Playboy* magazine.

ANTHONY LEWIS

୬୦ல

If there has been a theme in my life as a journalist, it has been a growing awareness of the danger of government power. In too many countries it was, and in some still is, totalitarian power.

The framers of our Constitution had an extraordinary understanding of the danger. They buttressed the republican system they created with checks and balances of power, and then they added the Bill of Rights to give specific protections to individuals. The courts have sometimes stood in the way of that abuse. But at other times, especially in war or national tension, the courts have deferred to official power.

That leaves a vigilant press as the last defense against tyranny. We have to keep trying—keep relearning what our essential duty is. As a reporter and columnist and essayist, I have been drawn to stories about the victims of official abuse: men and women fired as security risks in the McCarthy years without seeing the evidence; aliens long resident in the United States threatened with deportation because, years before, they had committed a crime as trivial as pulling another woman's hair. Did writing about these cases make a difference? Occasionally, yes; some people were saved. More profoundly, writing about the constitutional rights we are meant to have in this country can make Americans aware of those rights—and to demand them.

Racial segregation and discrimination are the great example. As the civil rights struggle was waged, reporters on the front line (not me; I was in Washington) made all Americans aware of the cruelty, the brutality, visited on black Americans for doing something as simple as trying to vote. The courts, in holding segregation unconstitutional, helped to inspire the civil rights movement. The press helped it to gain national support and, finally, to end official racism.

The evil is not always as obvious as racism. Presidents and attorneys general and lesser officials may mean well when they try to exercise power without any check on their actions. To the best of my one voice, I expect to go on resisting.

∞∞∞

ANTHONY LEWIS is a two-time Pulitzer Prize–winning columnist for the *New York Times*. He is the author of *Gideon's Trumpet* and *Make No Law*. He has also taught and lectured on journalism at Columbia and Harvard.

BILL MAHER

∞∞∞

What was *that* all about?

∞∞∞

BILL MAHER hosted the widely acclaimed program *Politically Incorrect with Bill Maher*. He now hosts the HBO series *Real Time with Bill Maher*.

〜о〜

Questioning the Answers

Much of life—the boring part—is answering questions. The askers get to us early. What is two plus two? Why aren't you eating your peas? Can you name the Ten Commandments?

Questions keep coming—in classrooms, living rooms, dining rooms—and then one day, a liberating one, it's realized that true living happens when you stop answering questions and begin questioning the answers.

America's militarists said in 2002 that a war budget of $355 billion—$11,000 a second or $972 million a day, which is four times more than the Peace Corps budget for a year—is not enough and must be increased if peace is to be won. I questioned that.

Some 40,000 people in the Third World die every day of hunger-related or preventable diseases, while in much of the First World a major preoccupation is searching for the best diet to lose weight. I questioned that.

High school history textbooks describe the feats of men who are peacebreakers—Caesar, Napoleon, Robert E. Lee, George Patton—but rarely the successes of women who are peacemakers: Dorothy Day, Emily Balch, Ginetta Sagan, Jody Williams, Jeannette Rankin. I questioned that.

For too long, I kept thinking that somebody should get to work to help create a peaceable society. Then I said, I'm somebody.

I didn't question that.

〜о〜

COLMAN McCARTHY, a former columnist for the *Washington Post*, directs the Center for Teaching Peace in Washington, DC. His most recent book is *I'd Rather Teach Peace*.

ROBERT NOVAK

～०∽

As my late partner, Rowland Evans, once said: "Whatever else I have been, I am a reporter." The obituary column I wrote about my late partner when he died in March 2001 was entitled: "Rowland Evans, Reporter." I would be honored by the same epitaph.

～०∽

ROBERT NOVAK is a political columnist. In addition to writing his nationally syndicated column, he has been affiliated with CNN since its inception in 1980. He currently hosts an interview show on CNN called *The Novak Zone*.

SALLY QUINN

～०∽

Good mother, good wife, good daughter, good friend.

～०∽

SALLY QUINN began her career as a reporter for the *Washington Post*, commenting on both the political and social aspects of Washington, DC. In 1998, she published *The Party: A Guide to Adventurous Entertaining*, offering readers tips on how to throw a successful party.

SALLY JESSY RAPHAEL

～∞～

Sally Jessy Raphael, noted radio personality and television talk-show host, died yesterday after a freak accident. The freak walked away unharmed. According to an unnamed, questionable source, the fatal accident occurred as Ms. Raphael was meeting with network broadcasting executives who told her they respected her experience and wisdom, and agreed completely with all her decision-making. It was at that moment that Ms. Raphael fell backward from her chair. The medical examiner confirmed they were unable to either revive her or to wipe the smile off her face.

Ms. Raphael is survived by her husband, who no longer has a viable source of income, her children, who look forward to the reading of the will, and her agent and lawyer, who do not know she's passed.

Ms. Raphael had long expressed the desire for a longer obituary recounting her many exploits in this world and others. However, given the short attention span of the reader, she knows she's lucky to get this.

～∞～

SALLY JESSY RAPHAEL is a journalist and former host of *The Sally Jessy Raphael Show*, which ran from 1985 until 2002.

GENE SHALIT

∽o∾

I won't be back after this message.

∽o∾

GENE SHALIT has been professionally reviewing films, books, and theater for over thirty-five years. Currently, he is a popular television personality as the film critic and arts editor for the NBC program *Today*.

MARIA SHRIVER

∽o∾

As a loving mom, wife, daughter, sister and friend.

∽o∾

MARIA SHRIVER is a journalist and contributing anchor for *Dateline NBC*. In 1998, she received a George Foster Peabody Award for her work on a documentary about Wisconsin's welfare reform program. Her children's books have gone on to become *New York Times* bestsellers.

LIZ SMITH

✎

Well, the great Dorothy Parker wanted, "Excuse My Dust!"
I would have to change mine to "Excuse My Dirt!"

✎

LIZ SMITH is a bestselling author and a syndicated gossip columnist. She
received an Emmy Award for reporting in 1995.

JOHN STOSSEL

✎

He fought for our liberty.

✎

JOHN STOSSEL has received nineteen Emmy Awards as a commentator
for *ABC News* and a correspondent for *20/20*. His special reports force
viewers to examine the social and political fabric of our times.

TED TURNER

✎

I have nothing more to say.

✎

TED TURNER is the founder of the Cable News Network (CNN) and
Turner Network Television (TNT). He is also a noted philanthropist.

GRETA VAN SUSTEREN

∽∘∾

Anything but O.J. Simpson or plastic surgery.

∽∘∾

GRETA VAN SUSTEREN began her career as a trial lawyer. In 1991, she launched her television career with CNN, covering the most notorious trials of the day. Currently, she is the host of Fox News Channel's *On the Record with Greta van Susteren*.

MIKE WALLACE

∽∘∾

Dear Larry—
Sorry I can't be more helpful, but—you see—I'm not going.

∽∘∾

MIKE WALLACE has been correspondent and co-editor of the CBS television program *60 Minutes* since its debut in 1968. Over the years, he has interviewed some of the most famous political and social figures.

CURTIS WILKIE

❦

I came home to be with my people.

—excerpted from *Dixie*

❦

CURTIS WILKIE began his career as a reporter while working in Mississippi during the civil rights movement. He went on to serve as a national and foreign correspondent for the *Boston Globe* for twenty-six years. His book, *Dixie: A Personal Odyssey through Events That Shaped the Modern South,* chronicles the profound changes that took place in his native South over the last fifty years.

Grand Finale

MUSICIANS AND SINGER-SONGWRITERS

꙳

EDDY ARNOLD

∽∘∾

I am almost late. I have retired.

∽∘∾

EDDY ARNOLD is one of the most popular country performers of the century. His singer-songwriter-guitarist career began in the mid-1930s and continued until he retired from performing in 1999. He was inducted into the Country Music Hall of Fame in 1966 and awarded the Country Music Association's first Entertainer of the Year Award in 1967.

PAT BOONE

∽∘∾

Pat Boone: Christian.
Address for Eternity: Heaven.

∽∘∾

PAT BOONE began his career as a popular music artist in the 1950s. In that decade, Boone's record sales were second only to those of Elvis Presley. A devout Christian, Boone changed his musical style in the late 1960s to become one of the most world-renowned Christian singer-songwriters. He is also known for his acting roles in both film and television and for his several books.

DEE DEE BRIDGEWATER

❧

A mother, a wife, a diva for life—she loved us, then left us, and how she bereft us. May she scat in peace boo-boop-dee-do. We love you.

❧

DEE DEE BRIDGEWATER is a two-time Grammy Award–winning singer. Her vocal styling begs comparison to the female jazz greats who were her role models, including Ella Fitzgerald and Billie Holiday. Bridgewater also achieved great success as an actress, receiving a Tony Award for her performance in Broadway's *The Wiz* and a Laurence Olivier Award for her performance in the London production of *Lady Day*.

DAVE BRUBECK

❧

I opened doors.

After giving it some serious thought I don't think I can improve on those three words, because I do think that is the most important work I have done in my life—open doors—musically, racially, socially, mentally, and spiritually.

❧

DAVE BRUBECK is an award-winning jazz pianist and classical composer. In 2000, he and his wife, Iola, opened the Brubeck Institute in conjunction with the University of the Pacific in California. The institute combines creative expression through jazz and classical music with an interdisciplinary education in social politics.

ERIC BURDON

❦

I lost my wife (actually I lost two of them). I lost my house. I lost my dog. And now I'm losing my mind. But that's okay, 'cause I'm giving it all to you. You can do what you want with it.

❦

ERIC BURDON is a rock and roll legend who was Inducted into the Rock and Roll Hall of Fame in 1994 along with the other members of his former band, the Animals.

DEANA CARTER

❦

You either make dust, or eat dust. There is no in between.

❦

DEANA CARTER is an award-winning country music singer. Her first album, *I Shaved My Legs for This?*, went platinum.

ROY CLARK

❦

God knows, I tried.

❦

ROY CLARK is perhaps best known for his guitar playing and songwriting ability. The host of the television show *Hee Haw* for twenty-five years, Clark is also an accomplished actor.

HAL DAVID

❦

What's it all about, Hal?

I'd like to be remembered for the lyrics that I wrote. They seemed to have lasted through the years, so I guess they touched people's hearts, and were meaningful enough for them not only to be remembered by those who heard them when they were new—but to have been rediscovered over the years by younger listeners and performers alike.

People often wrote to tell me that they remembered important milestones in their lives because of one of my songs. They proposed to their best girl to one of my lyrics, they celebrated anniversaries with one of my lyrics, they sang their babies to sleep by singing one of my lyrics.

That touched my heart, and meant a great deal to me.

❦

HAL DAVID is an Academy Award– and Grammy Award–winning lyricist whose songs are some of the most famous known today. He is responsible for such timeless classics as "Raindrops Keep Falling on My Head," "Don't Make Me Over," "The Look of Love," and "Walk on By." Three of his songs are in the Grammy Hall of Fame and three others have received Academy Award nominations.

CHIP DAVIS

If

If my music has reawakened feelings in people
If my music has sensitized people to nature
If my music makes children dance
I have done my job on this earth as a composer.

CHIP DAVIS is the founding member of the award-winning group Mannheim Steamroller. This Grammy Award–winning composer and musician, whose albums have sold more than 36 million copies worldwide, developed a unique blend of classical music and electronic rock.

KEVIN EUBANKS

I sit in the well of the wave
Being stirred by the Moon
Touching neither Earth nor Air
I dance within the turn of Life
And drift on the seas of forever.

KEVIN EUBANKS is a prolific and award-winning jazz guitarist who is currently the music director for *The Tonight Show with Jay Leno*.

CONNIE FRANCIS

✥

Show business has afforded me a lifetime filled with high-points and exhilaration I never would have experienced in any other walk of life. It also exposed me to many low points and hazards. I would like to be remembered not so much for the heights I have reached but for the depths from which I have risen.

✥

CONNIE FRANCIS is one of the most successful female recording artists of all time. She is known as a master of interpretation, able to infuse any song she sings with emotion. At points during her extensive career, she sang songs in many different languages, including Italian, French, German, and Hebrew.

ART GARFUNKEL

✥

Always with love, Art Garfunkel.

✥

ART GARFUNKEL began singing with friend and partner Paul Simon at the young age of eleven. They went on to win five Grammy Awards together. Garfunkel has since taken on extensive solo work as a musician and written several books. He is also known for his famous Walk Across America and other long-distance walks.

DEBORAH GIBSON

❧

To be read to guests attending my celebration of life:

I hope I have passed with a smile on my face that conveys how truly blessed my life has been. I hope that people will, years from now, continue to slow dance to my music at weddings and sing "Electric Youth" into a hairbrush with wild abandon—*that* is the point of the music I have made. I hope I, in some way, have contributed to making both friends' and strangers' lives a little brighter. I hope that I am seated at the right hand of The Father, The King, and . . . Liberace. I want to be remembered most of all as a kind spirit.

Anyone can be a self-centered star. Preserving the integrity of the soul takes work. I look back on my life, thankful for being carried by an incredible quartet—God, family, friends, and music. This quartet, in perfect harmony, has made it a thrill to be alive. I refer now to a lyric from the musical *Les Miserables*: "To love another person is to see the face of God." I have seen God again and again; I don't know any other meaning to this journey.

To all attending this celebration of life—always dance to the song that's in your heart and you will never tire. No regrets, only lessons. And, hey—thanks for being here!! Now go enjoy the food.

❧

DEBORAH GIBSON is an award-winning singer-songwriter whose breakout hits "Electric Youth" and "Lost in Your Eyes" have earned her a place among America's most recognized cultural icons. She has appeared on Broadway and in other musical theater. She continues to write and record music.

BERRY GORDY JR.

❧

A teacher; one who loved and was loved.

❧

BERRY GORDY JR. is the founder and owner of the Tamla-Motown family record labels. He established Motown Records as one of the most important independent labels in the early 1960s.

DENYCE GRAVES

❧

She used life to express and create who she was. She was song.

❧

DENYCE GRAVES is a world-renowned operatic singer who has performed to sold-out audiences all around the world. Some of her most notable performances include the role of Carmen in *Carmen* and Dalila in *Samson et Dalila*.

SAMMY HAGAR

∽◦∾

I think just to be remembered would be a fine thing. But for how long? Now that's the question.

∽◦∾

SAMMY HAGAR is a rock and roll legend who was, for many years, the lead singer of Van Halen. His numerous solo albums have all been major sellers.

JERRY HERMAN

∽◦∾

I would like to be remembered as "That guy who made us hum on the way out of the theater."

∽◦∾

JERRY HERMAN is a lyricist and composer who created the scores for such famous musicals as *Hello, Dolly!* and *La Cage Aux Folles*.

MARILYN HORNE

❧

And for my encore . . .

❧

MARILYN HORNE is a world-renowned concert and opera singer. She founded the Marilyn Horne Foundation to support and preserve the art of the vocal recital.

BRUCE HORNSBY

❧

With uneven ears and pipe in hand, with sandwiches conveniently at hand, he was a strong swimmer in the sea of actual circumstances.

❧

BRUCE HORNSBY is a multi-platinum-selling recording artist. His expressive piano, on such lasting hits as "The Way It Is," has brought him his most enduring fame. He is also known for his willingness to experiment with other instruments and for his lyricism. He has played and co-written with many musical greats such as the Grateful Dead, Bonnie Raitt, Bob Dylan, and Don Henley.

JANIS IAN

∞◇∞

This is what happened when she stopped talking.

∞◇∞

JANIS IAN began her music career with her thought-provoking album, *Society's Child*, when she was only fifteen. She has since released over fifteen albums and been honored with multiple Grammy Awards. The first musical performer on *Saturday Night Live*, she is also known for her opinion columns in various publications.

DAVID JONES

∞◇∞

"You'll miss me when I'm gone," was heard from my father on many humorous occasions. "They'll have to give me a shot to put me away." More laughter. And, "Oh, dad. Mum. Oh, Harry, shut up." And finally as they carried him up to the ambulance, "I'm a goner, son."

I will be on my feet when you remember me. Freedom fighting, angry little man, full of piss and vinegar. The world's greatest entertainer. Funny, ha! Loyal, outspoken, father, brother, friend. All forgiven, agreed, forgotten. You will remember me for I will never leave you. I will always be in your life. I receive you and support you, I am going ahead.

∞◇∞

DAVID JONES was a member of the popular band the Monkees and has performed in numerous guest appearances on television.

JULIUS LA ROSA

❧

Wisdom

Thirty years ago I got a phone call from a dear friend; a lady of great sensitivity and intelligence who was a kind of surrogate aunt. I recorded the call in my Book of Memories.

So—what are friends for? Dorothy wasn't on the phone ten seconds and I knew she was upset. I listened and let her get everything off her considerable chest, her frustration peaking with a not untypical and oh, so Italian, "And when I die, I want them to put on my stone, 'She put up the good fight!'"

She was finished. It was my turn.

And when I die, I want them to say, "All his life he tried to be an honest man."

"But Julie, you're one of the most honest men I know! Who do you consider an honest man?"

"Christopher," I said, my four-year-old son.

"Julie," she responded, "Don't confuse honesty with innocence." And like Oscar Hammerstein said, "All the rest is talk!"

❧

JULIUS LA ROSA is a recording artist, singer, and entertainer.

CHRISTINE LAVIN

❧

The two biggest influences on Ms. Lavin's career were legendary bluesman guitarist Dave Van Ronk and Australian megastar-humanitarian Dame Edna. The last years of her life Christine was convinced that Dame Edna was her birth mother, though DNA tests run by the law firm of Barry Scheck proved inconclusive [Dame Edna could not be reached for comment].

At the time of her death, Christine was set to record her next collection of songs tantalizingly entitled *Bad Girl Trapped in a Good Girl's Body* and her new weight-loss feng shui workout video, *Lunch Ladies Gone Wild*. She leaves behind dozens of heartbroken fans, 15 solo albums, 8 brothers and sisters, 11 nieces and nephews, 48 cousins, 2 stunned boyfriends, and one 625 sq. ft. cozy, quiet one-bedroom apartment in a doorman building on Riverside Drive (Wake Bros. Realty, 212.KL5.4321, open house this Sunday).

∞○∞

CHRISTINE LAVIN is a singer-songwriter. She has released over fifteen albums and won numerous awards. She has helped many singersongwriters get their start by producing their songs on compilation albums and organizing workshops on performance, such as her Martha's Vineyard Singer/Songwriters' Retreat.

TOMMY LEE

∞○∞

We get one chance to rock in this lifetime so why not do it flying?

I've made a few mistakes, but I hope that some folks can learn from my mistakes or take a lesson, you know, like don't try this at home! Falling in love, playing music, traveling the world, finding your spiritual nature, raising kids and enjoying the wonders of the world, that's what my life was about.

I hope I made an impression on people I met during that journey, hope they felt they had encountered someone that enjoyed life. I've had plenty of speed bumps on the highway to Heaven (don't talk to me about that other place; I saw the brochure. No thanks!).

On the road of life there are passengers and there are drivers. Well, I'm wearing my fireproof race suit. Now where's the gas pedal? I'm floorin' it! And don't worry, I'm wearing my seatbelt!

∽✺∾

TOMMY LEE is one of the best-known rock and roll stars of our time. His energy and passion for playing the drums were a perfect complement to his band, Mötley Crüe. In the 1990s, Lee went on to explore other aspects of heavy metal music, both with other bands and through solo efforts.

RANDY NEWMAN

∽✺∾

I'm not angry, just disappointed.

∽✺∾

RANDY NEWMAN is an Academy Award–winning composer and musician. He has composed the scores for many films, including the easily recognizable theme from the film *Parenthood*, entitled "I Love to See You Smile." He also composed a musical version of Goethe's famous book *Faust*.

HERB REED

❧

I would like to be remembered as the man and the bass singer who created one of the most popular singing groups in the world, "The Platters." I didn't live a perfect life, but I always lived an honest one. I was one of many that had to overcome the civil rights movement, and had every right to be bitter because of what I endured. However, I felt like I was always a good friend to many and always gave something back to those in need. As I write this, I know during my lifetime I have been mistreated and taken advantage of, but God knows who those people are and they will someday be judged by Him.

I hope the music of "the Platters" lives on long after I am gone and continues to inspire both the young and the old alike.

❧

HERB REED is the original founder of the Platters. In 1990, Herb Reed and the Platters were inducted into the Rock and Roll Hall of Fame.

KENNY ROGERS

❧

A Life

If you look upon life's journey
As a single day in life
You'll spend half your time in darkness
And the other half in light.

If in the early morning hours
When the sun comes breaking through
That life's colors, shapes and shadows
Have the most to offer you.

When the sun is at its brightest
And its heat is in your eyes
It's hard to know which road to take
Or where your future lies.

It's just as hard to see in total white
As it is in total black
But it's harder yet to see that
'til you're past and looking back.

But there's beauty in the sunset
As the colors fade away
It's God's gift to those who persevere
Through the bright part of the day.

And as you watch the sunset
You'll feel better if you know
When you reach your darkest hour
There's a better place you go.

Written as a gift for my son, Christopher,
on November 22, 1996.

KENNY ROGERS is a country music legend. Over the course of his career, he has released nearly sixty albums and received four Grammy Awards. In 1998, Rogers co-wrote, scored, and starred in an off-Broadway musical. He is also known for his continuing efforts to help America's homeless and for his work as a professional photographer. His famous song "The Gambler" is just as popular today as it was when it was originally released.

NED ROREM

❦

He became immortal and then he died.

❦

NED ROREM is a prolific composer who has worked in nearly every genre, focusing on orchestral music and music for the stage. He has received numerous honors, including a Fulbright Fellowship (1951) and a Guggenheim Fellowship (1957). He is also the accomplished author of fourteen books.

NEIL SEDAKA

❦

The creative person always had to struggle with issues, and always had a cross to bear. I felt things to a greater degree than other people. Many times I lived through my art and music, realizing that life can be cruel. I painted lyrics and music of beauty and fantasy, a world far better than our real world. I hope my work will go on long after me, perhaps giving hope and joy to others. I tried to take people away from fears and depression in this crazy world. We only have fleeting moments of happiness.

I had no secrets. I found it difficult to play mind games with others. People had to like me as I was. I couldn't always please others all the time, though I tried desperately. Finally, in the end, I had to please myself.

I was fun to be around. A nice person, caring and sensitive. I was passive and sometimes a pushover. But if someone crossed me, I would reject their friendship. Being an artist, I would think with my heart and not my head.

I had a wonderful family, and good friends. I have no regrets.

∾◦∾

NEIL SEDAKA began his career in the 1950s, composing music with lyricist Howard Greenfield. His first major songwriting success, "Stupid Cupid," allowed him to enjoy a career as a singer throughout the 1950s and into today.

ARTIE SHAW

∾◦∾

I truly don't care how I'm remembered; all I want to do is hang around as long as possible. After that, if someone feels I really must have a headstone (or some other marker) on my grave, let them have just two words carved on it: Go Away.

∾◦∾

ARTIE SHAW began performing at age fifteen. He was well known across the industry for his unique and expressive jazz clarinet, but is perhaps best known as one of the most famous big band leaders of the 1930s. He has also written several books.

BEVERLY SILLS

❧

The best is yet to come.

❧

BEVERLY SILLS is an opera singer and performer who began touring at age fifteen. She is also the National Chair of the March of Dimes' Mothers March on Birth Defects.

VIENNA TENG

❧

Passage

I died in a car crash
Two days ago
Was unrecognizable
When they pulled me from the gears
No one's fault, no one's bottle
No one's teenage pride or throttle
Our innocence is all the worse for fears
The other walked away alive
Arms wrapped now around his wife

My lover sits, the silent eye
In a hurricane of warmth and word
My mother trembles with the sobs
Whose absence seems absurd
My sister shouts to let her see

Through the cloud of crowd surrounding me
My colleagues call for silence in my name

I died in a car crash
Three months ago
They burned me 'til I glowed
And crumbled to a fine gray sand
Now I am nothing
Everywhere
Several breaths of strangers' air
And all thoughts ever written in my hand
They plant my tree out in the yard
It grows, but takes the winter hard

My lover puts a knife to wrist
Says
"Tomorrow comes; hold on a while."
My mother tosses in the sheets
And dreams me holding my own child
My sister plays our homemade tapes
Laughs as tears stream down her face
My office door now wears a different name

I died in a car crash
Four years ago
My tree drinks melted snow
Just eight feet tall, a pale and fragile thing
Bee stings—beaches—bright vacations—
Sunburnt high school graduations—
A sparrow healing from a broken wing
This year, a glimpse of second chances:
Tiny apples on my tree's branches

My lover hears the open wind
And crawls blinking into the sun

My mother leafs through photographs
Like memories the colors run
My sister can't decide her truth
Asks aloud what I might do
In a conference hall, my brief efforts engraved

I died in a car crash
A lifetime ago it seems
Been a decade or two or three
They've just released a new design
Bars and bags front and behind
My fate now an impossibility
Safely packaged, hurtling down
The highway hardly makes a sound

My lover very much alive
Arms wrapped now around his wife

—from the album *Feather Moon*.
Words and music® 2001, Vienna Teng

VIENNA TENG is a singer-songwriter. At only six years old, she began composing music for the piano and now releases albums of her compositions. Influenced by a multitude of musical genres, Teng's music infuses intricate piano sounds with unique vocals.

ANDY WILLIAMS

∽∾∽

"Moon River"
Thank God I didn't record "Why Don't We Do It in the Road."

∽∾∽

ANDY WILLIAMS's career as a vocalist is one of the longest lasting of his era. From 1963 to 1972, he hosted *The Andy Williams Show*, which won three Emmy Awards. One of his most popular songs, "Moon River," won an Academy Award. Williams still performs today at a theater he built in Branson, Missouri.

OTIS WILLIAMS

∽∾∽

People used to ask me, "How long will the Temptations continue?"

And I would say, "I'm going to ride the hair off the horse until it is bald!"

Now that I am unemployed, I hope that God lets me into heaven.

∽∾∽

OTIS WILLIAMS is one of the founding members of the classic Motown group the Temptations. His presence and perseverance helped lead the Temptations to numerous hit songs such as "My Girl."

ROGER WILLIAMS

❦

There *is* something beyond.

❦

ROGER WILLIAMS began playing piano at the very young age of three.
He went on to become the largest-selling piano recording artist in history.

A Hard
Act to
Follow

PERFORMERS AND ENTERTAINERS

〜〜〜

TAMMY FAYE BAKKER

✌∽

I have fought the good fight; I have finished the race; I have kept the faith. Finally, there is laid up for me the crown of righteousness, which the Lord, the righteous Judge, will give me on that day, and not to me only but also to all who have loved His appearing.

—2 Timothy 4: 7–8

✌∽

TAMMY FAYE BAKKER is a televangelist, author, and performer. As a minister, she has helped develop many Christian television networks. Bakker has also released twenty-five musical albums.

BOB BARKER

✌∽

Instead of sending flowers, please have your pets spayed or neutered!

✌∽

BOB BARKER is the host of *The Price Is Right*, America's longest-running game show. He received the Daytime Emmy Lifetime Achievement Award in 1999.

DAVID COPPERFIELD

∽∘∾

This time I won't be reappearing in the middle of the audience.

I get to Heaven and Moses won't leave me alone with the "My miracles are bigger than yours" bit. By the way, he looks nothing like Chuck Heston, but he's a dead ringer for P. Diddy.

I talked to the Big Guy. Says he hates suspenders.

∽∘∾

DAVID COPPERFIELD is a magician and performer who has delighted audiences around the world with his daring escapes and dazzling stunts.

RICK DEES

∽∘∾

I'll see you in heaven, if you're caller Number 100 at 555–1027.

∽∘∾

RICK DEES is the host of the radio program *Rick Dees Weekly Top 40,* which is heard on more than five hundred radio stations worldwide. He was inducted into the Radio Hall of Fame in 1999.

JOHN EDWARD

✌⊙∾

He knew his voice was just a whisper, and hoped that someone might have heard.

He always said, "If in my life, just one person was helped by my work, than it was *all* worth it."

He hoped the reality was millions instead.

✌⊙∾

JOHN EDWARD is a medium, author, and lecturer. He is the host of *Crossing Over with John Edward*, a widely syndicated television program in which he helps his audience communicate with lost loved ones.

EDNA EVERAGE

✌⊙∾

The story of the late Dame Edna Everage is one of the most moving and inspirational of our time. She was born Edna May Beazley to a pioneering Australian family in the Outback town of Wagga Wagga at a date she was always too modest to reveal in case admirers around the world flooded her with unwelcome gifts they could not afford.

She is an important and enduring figure in the cultural life of the late 20th Century and early Millennium and a high female achiever in the ranks of Thatcher, Madonna, Streisand, Mother Teresa, and Martha Stewart. Myths surround her life and work and it has even been whispered that she is still alive and well in her luxurious compound in the Australian Outback planning a fresh assault on American culture.

∽∘∾

DAME EDNA is a cultural icon who has given Tony Award–winning performances on Broadway, written numerous books, and is also a noted philanthropist.

MERV GRIFFIN

∽∘∾

So lately, in idle moments, I've been toying with what I'd like my headstone to read. (You don't think I'm going to let anybody *else* write my last line, do you?)

There's always the hypochondriac's epitaph: "I *told* you I was sick." Or perhaps the talk show host's final exit line would be more appropriate: "I will *not* be right back after this message."

Hey, you know what? I've just figured out what I want to say:

"Stay tuned."

—excerpted from *Merv: Making the Good Life Last*

∽∘∾

MERV GRIFFIN was the host of the Emmy Award–winning television program *The Merv Griffin Show*. He is also the creator of two of the most popular game shows of all time, *Wheel of Fortune* and *Jeopardy!*

MONTY HALL

~o~

I had a terrific life—marriage, family—my career and my charity work. How this will be remembered and validated is up to those I leave behind.

~o~

MONTY HALL co-created and hosted the hit television game show *Let's Make a Deal*. He has made numerous guest appearances on a variety of popular television programs, including *The Love Boat, The Wonder Years,* and *The Nanny*.

GRAHAM KERR

~o~

I tried and then I tried again, like a salmon heading upstream in spite of, or perhaps because of, the waterfalls and the occasional bears and now, by the grace of God, I'm home.

~o~

GRAHAM KERR is an expert on nutrition and healthful eating. His television cooking shows have offered viewers healthy recipes for over thirty years. He is the author of over twenty books.

THE AMAZING KRESKIN

❦

Even now, I know what you're thinking!

❦

THE AMAZING KRESKIN is a nationally known mentalist who, while not a psychic, is able to read people's thoughts. He is the author of ten books, including *The Amazing World of Kreskin* and *Use Your Head to Get Ahead!*

FRANCES LANGFORD

❦

Please remember me as a simple person, who loved this country, its people and especially its military servicemen and women. Our servicemen needed us and we were there. I will always consider it one of the greatest honors of my life to have entertained the troops during the war years with Bob Hope and the USO.

❦

FRANCES LANGFORD got her start in vaudeville theater in the late 1920s. She began her work with Bob Hope in 1941 on his radio show, *Pepsodent*. She went on to travel the globe with Hope, entertaining troops during World War II.

ROBIN LEACH

∾o∾

Hi, this is Robin Leach standing outside the pearly gates!

∾o∾

ROBIN LEACH was the executive producer, host, and writer for the hit television series *Lifestyles of the Rich and Famous*.

ART LINKLETTER

∾o∾

No could've
No would've
No should've ·
I did and went happily!

∾o∾

ART LINKLETTER is an Emmy and Grammy Award–winning entertainer who has performed in such popular television and radio shows as *House Party* and *Kids Say the Darndest Things*.

ED McMAHON

❦

I don't plan to have a headstone. I hope to be floating in the sea . . . but if I had a headstone my epitaph would be: "He was a good broadcaster and a great Marine!"

❦

ED McMAHON starred on *The Tonight Show with Johnny Carson* for almost thirty years and is currently the host of the popular television talent contest *Star Search*. McMahon served his country in both World War II and the Korean War as a pilot in the U.S. Marine Corps.

SYDNEY OMARR

❦

He was handsome, erudite and enjoyed boxing. But his star rose when he fought the good fight for astrology!

❦

SYDNEY OMARR was a world-renowned astrologist whose books on astrology have sold over 50 million copies. He passed away on January 2, 2003.

YOKO ONO

~o~

Imagine!

~o~

YOKO ONO began her career as a performance artist in the late 1950s. In the 1960s, she began releasing popular and experimental music albums. She is the widow of John Lennon.

GARY OWENS

~o~

Mispronounced dead on arrival!

~o~

GARY OWENS got his start, like many famous performers, on *Rowan and Martin's Laugh-In*. He has one of today's most widely recognized voices of, and has lent his voice to, over three thousand cartoons, including *Bobby's World*. He has made starring and guest appearances on dozens of television shows and has been inducted into both the Radio and Television Halls of Fame.

CLAUDIA SCHIFFER

Writing my eulogy at thirty-two is really too early considering the best years of my life are hopefully still to come. My biggest wish is to be the perfect mother to my child and wife to my husband. My deepest regret would be to outlive my children and my greatest hope is that modern medicine will help me live to see my great-grandchildren.

And that's all I can report right now.

Ask me again in fifty years.

PS: *Nihil de mortuis nisi bene.*

CLAUDIA SCHIFFER is a German-born supermodel who is internationally recognized for her extraordinary beauty and grace.

Term

Limits

**POLITICIANS, PUBLIC FIGURES,
AND ACTIVISTS**

GLORIA ALLRED

My life has been dedicated to helping to improve the status and conditions of women and minorities by asserting, protecting, and vindicating their rights in courts of law and in the court of public opinion. My goal has been to win the achievement of equal rights for women with men under the law, and freedom from discrimination for those who are denied it. My efforts have been focused on improving the lives of those who have been the victims of injustice, and I have worked in a public way to right the wrongs against them, with the hope that it would inspire and teach others so that they can find their own strength and courage to fight back and win the rights to which they are entitled, but which they have often been denied.

I have worked to win tougher enforcement of child support laws; more rights for rape victims; more protection for battered women, rights for pregnant women to be free of job discrimination; continuation of women's legal right to choose abortion; freedom from sexual harassment in the workplace; more rights and protection for children who have been sexually abused; and rights for those who have been discriminated against on account of their sex, race, age, or sexual orientation in the workplace.

My final words are the words of the famous labor organizer Mother Jones, who once said, "Pray for the dead, and fight like hell for the living."

I will miss you, but I will also know that in death at last we are all equal!

GLORIA ALLRED is an attorney and radio talk-show host in Los Angeles, California. Over the years she has made many legal advances for women, minorities, and others who face discrimination.

ERIN BROCKOVICH-ELLIS

The greatest gift I ever received was the smile on my child's face or even the smile of someone I did not know because I cared, gave my time to them or said something as simple as "You look nice today."

Remember me when I am gone as the person who gave a damn!

ERIN BROCKOVICH-ELLIS is a champion for consumer rights and an advocate for environmental causes.

JEB BUSH

I hope that when I am gone, people who choose to remember me would say that I worked hard at whatever I did, and that my greatest joy was centered around my family. If I am remembered first and foremost as a dad and a husband, then I think you could say I kept my priorities straight.

JEB BUSH is the governor of Florida.

MARGARETHE CAMMERMEYER

❦

Living to its fullest has been my reality in life. As my parents' gun runner when I was two months old, as a soldier in my mid-years, and an activist in later life, my dream was to take a stand, to make a difference, to change the world. The older I got the more idiosyncratic I became, less concerned about tradition and more concerned about challenging the system. It was always important to push the limits, my own and those of others. Every time life settled down or it was time to retire, there was a call from within to do something, anything. It seemed a shame to have had extraordinary life experiences and not to use them for a greater good. In retirement there were new careers, more upheavals, more change and more growth. My dreams became reality because my partner, children, grandchildren, friends and extended family were the enablers; they nurtured, supported, taunted and challenged and knew there was never a limit to possibility. Don't dare to tell me it can't be done! I'll prove you wrong. Underdogs win when the cause is right. If you are uncomfortable it is where you need to be.

❦

COLONEL MARGARETHE CAMMERMEYER has served as an army nurse and is a recipient of the Bronze Star. She is a groundbreaking activist in the area of gay rights in the military and the author of *Serving in Silence*.

ALAN DERSHOWITZ

He was never boring.

He said out loud what others whispered.

He challenged authority; the higher the authority, the stronger the challenge.

He made the legal system more accessible to the public.

He taught thousands of students and educated even more readers and viewers.

He listened best with his mouth open.

He was fun to be with.

He was never boring.

All this, without knowing how to use a computer.

ALAN M. DERSHOWITZ is a professor of law at Harvard University. He is a bestselling author who has been profiled by every major magazine in America.

BOB DOLE

I demand a recount.

SENATOR BOB DOLE has been the chairman of the Republican National Committee, both Senate majority and minority leader, and chairman of the Senate Finance Committee. He is also a recipient of the Presidential Medal of Freedom, the highest civilian award in government.

MARIAN WRIGHT EDELMAN

∽੦∼

There is a quote by Bertolt Brecht I love—

> *There are those who struggle for a day*
> *And they are good*
> *There are those who struggle for a year*
> *And they are better*
> *There are those who struggle all their lives*
> *These are the indispensable ones.*

I hope to be counted as one of the indispensable ones who struggled to truly Leave No Child Behind.

∽੦∼

MARIAN WRIGHT EDELMAN is a lawyer, educator, activist, reformer, and children's advocate. She is the founder and president of the Children's Defense Fund and was the first African American woman admitted to the Mississippi state bar.

JOHN EISENHOWER

∽੦∼

He followed his own career as a military writer. It meant far more to him than his distinguished ancestry.

∽੦∼

JOHN S. D. EISENHOWER is a military historian as well as the author of several bestselling books.

BARNEY FRANK

❦

At this point I have spent nearly half of my entire life—and most of my adult life—as a member of the House of Representatives, and I expect to be doing this for at least another ten years. The part of the job which I have most enjoyed has been the give and take of debates where members engage in serious and spontaneous discussion of issues. In this process, when one has finished his participation in a particular discussion, and another member seeks to continue that discussion, the phrase uttered by the presiding officer to note that the individual in question has completed his contribution to the debate is the phrase I choose:

The gentleman has yielded.

❦

CONGRESSMAN BARNEY FRANK has served in Congress since 1981. He represents the Fourth District of Massachusetts.

JOHN GAVIN

❦

Oh my, another career change!

❦

JOHN GAVIN was a stage, screen, and television star in the 1950s. He later served as United States ambassador to Mexico, a post he held from 1981 to 1986.

PHYLLIS GEORGE

∽o∾

First Lady of Sports
First Lady of Kentucky
First Lady of Chicken
First Lady of Inspiration

∽o∾

PHYLLIS GEORGE is a former Miss America and the First Lady of Kentucky. She is also the author of a number of books, including *Never Say Never: Ten Lessons to Turn You Can't into Yes I Can*.

ALEXANDER HAIG

∽o∾

He Really Was In Charge

∽o∾

ALEXANDER HAIG JR. is a four-star general and former secretary of state.

ORRIN HATCH

❦

He got things done.

❦

ORRIN G. HATCH has served as senator from Utah since 1976.

ERNEST HOLLINGS

❦

He either fears his fate too much,
Or his deserts are small,
That puts it not unto the touch
To win or lose it all.

—James Graham, Marquis of Montrose

❦

ERNEST F. HOLLINGS is the senator from South Carolina and has
served on a variety of government committees.

ROY INNIS

܁܁

I would like to be remembered as one who persevered, despite obvious, palpable, invidious censorship by much of the media (both black and white) of my ideas.

Despite that, friends and honest foes could not deny that I was committed to the principles of Truth, Logic, Courage (TLC) and Fairness.

܁܁

ROY INNIS is the national chairman of the Congress of Racial Equality (CORE).

FRANK KEATING

܁܁

The Anti Epitaph

What happened to the calendar,
And all those months and years?
What happened to the sunsets,
And all those unseen skies?
What happened to those New Year's Resolutions,
And all those missed trips and unread books?
What happened to the Golden Rule, and love of
*   neighbor,*
And all those unmet needs and too few hugs?
I never missed a meal, but I missed a lot of good meals.
I never missed a laugh, but I missed a lot of good laughs.

I rarely missed work, but I didn't always do my best work.
I should have taken fewer naps;
Lived each day breathing in great gulps of God's good air;
Spent more time building sand castles instead of worrying
   about the sea.
But it's over and I'm not coming back.
Tough.

∽o∾

FRANK KEATING is the president and CEO of the American Council of
Life Insurers and the former governor of Oklahoma.

HENRY KISSINGER

∽o∾

April 23, 2029

The nation is in mourning for the passing of Henry Alfred
Kissinger, America's most revered statesman, who died unex-
pectedly yesterday at the age of 106.

In government and in private life, his service to his adopted
country was extraordinary: Secretary of State, National Security Advisor, Chair of numerous Presidential Commissions and
NGOs, professor, philanthropist, author, lecturer, commentator, columnist, geopolitical consultant. The office of President
was denied him, due to his foreign birth, and he always dis-
couraged attempts by his fellow citizens to alter the
Constitution.

Kissinger was also known for his modesty, his even tem-
perament (no present or former staff member is able to recall
an instance when he raised his voice in frustration or anger),

194

his wit, his accent-less English, his trim figure and his ability to sleep on airplanes. When asked a few years ago what, if any, were the advantages of his advanced years, he replied, "I seem to have outlived everyone who ever attacked me."

He is survived by his wife, Nancy, ninety-five, two children, four grandchildren, twelve great-grandchildren, and fifty great-great-grandchildren, all of whom are budding geniuses with curly hair. The family has requested that, in lieu of flowers and testimonials, memorial donations be made to The Kissinger Foundation to Aid Labrador Retrievers or to The Kissinger Foundation for the Development of a Winning U.S. World Cup Soccer Team.

∞◦∞

HENRY KISSINGER is one of the most influential political figures alive today. He has served in public office for the majority of his adult life.

EDWARD KOCH

∞◦∞

He was fiercely proud of his Jewish faith. He fiercely defended the City of New York and he fiercely loved the people of the City of New York.

—Ed Koch, *I'm Not Done Yet*

∞◦∞

EDWARD KOCH was the mayor of New York City from 1978 to 1989. He is a renowned commentator and the author of twelve books.

JOSEPH LIEBERMAN

❦

Born in Connecticut. Raised in Connecticut. Educated in Connecticut. Elected in Connecticut. Knew his way around Connecticut.

Loving son, brother, husband, father, grandfather, and friend.

Served God and country with purpose and pleasure.

Lucky to live in the greatest country ever created, he did his best to make it better.

❦

SENATOR JOSEPH LIEBERMAN has served three terms in the United States Senate as a delegate from Connecticut.

EUGENE McCARTHY

❦

In 1968 he was campaigning at a college in Chicago, and was in an auditorium with a plastic roof. Unfortunately, it was hailing and he said, "It was like giving a speech in a drum!" It would stop hailing, and he would resume his speech. Then it would start hailing again and he would stop. This happened three times, and on the third time he said, "Don't worry; I can hear myself."

He said he would like that as his epitaph: "Don't worry; I can hear myself."

❦

SENATOR EUGENE MCCARTHY served as a member of Congress, in both the House of Representatives and the Senate, from 1949 until 1971.

OLIVER NORTH

I have fought the good fight, I have finished the race, I have kept the faith.

OLIVER NORTH is a prominent political statesman, decorated military officer, and the author of several books.

ROSS PEROT

I would like to be remembered for:

- Being born in the greatest country in the history of man—the United States of America, and in this country's greatest state—Texas!
- Having the finest parents and sister any boy could ever hope for.
- Having the world's most wonderful wife, Margot.
- Having five outstanding children—Ross, Nancy, Suzanne, Carolyn, and Katherine—all of whom have become world-class parents.

- Having fifteen *perfect grandchildren* (with more possibly on the way).
- My boyhood friends and neighbors—who were great role models.
- My outstanding ministers, Sunday school teachers, public school teachers, Cub Scout and Boy Scout leaders who urged all of the children to be honest, trustworthy and loyal, and to "Reach for the Stars" and "Dream the Impossible Dream."
- The opportunity to attend the U.S. Naval Academy and be associated with outstanding young men from all fifty states.
- Being taught leadership and being required to maintain the highest standards of honor and integrity in the Navy.
- The great people I had the privilege to be associated with during my four years at sea after graduation from the Naval Academy.
- The opportunity to travel around the world on a Navy Destroyer through twenty-two foreign countries and seventeen seas and oceans.
- All of the incredibly talented, dedicated people who made my companies and civic activities successful.
- Colonel Simons and the Iranian rescue team.
- All of my great friends who have brought joy, happiness and support throughout my life.

To paraphrase Abraham Lincoln, All I am, or ever hope to be, I owe to these wonderful people.

You are the wind beneath my wings—I would have been nothing without you!

Thank you for a wonderful life!

ROSS PEROT is a Texas billionaire who launched a campaign for the presidency on the Reform Party ticket in 1992.

ANN RICHARDS

∞∞∞

She did her damnedest.

∞∞∞

ANN RICHARDS is a former governor of Texas. As governor, she appointed many women and minorities to state positions, thus increasing the options available for these minorities.

PAT SCHROEDER

∞∞∞

She tried her darnedest and outlived a lot of enemies!

∞∞∞

PAT SCHROEDER is the president and CEO of the Association of American Publishers. She is also a former member of the U.S. Congress.

DONNA SHALALA

꩜

If you remember me at all, remember me simply as a good citizen of this country—as a patriot who loves her country and who served it well.

꩜

DONNA SHALALA served as secretary of health and human services for the United States government and is currently the president of the University of Miami.

PAUL SIMON

꩜

Because my first wife died several years ago, my tombstone is already prepared. It reads simply: Paul Simon. I do want my grandchildren to know a little about me, and I hope they can be proud of me. But beyond that I am less concerned with being remembered than in leaving a legacy of having given an opportunity to those who lack it. My political mentor, Senator Paul Douglas, said he did not worry about the rich and powerful. They can take care of themselves, and too often government caters to their whims. He was correct. We need to help those who struggle for the basics in life, in this nation and in other countries. To the extent we sit comfortably aloof from their problems, we endanger the future of my grandchildren and their grandchildren. To the extent that we combine compassion with action and wisdom, we create a world of peace and justice and opportunity for all humanity. I want to contribute to that dream, whether anyone remembers me for it or not.

∽๑∾

PAUL SIMON served as United States Senator from Illinois and later founded and directed the Public Policy Institute at Southern Illinois University. He passed away on December 9, 2003.

JESSE VENTURA

∽๑∾

Loved His Wife. Loved His Family. Loved His Country. They Loved Him Back.

∽๑∾

JESSE VENTURA is a former professional wrestler and bodybuilder and also served as governor of Minnesota.

TOM VILSACK

∽๑∾

It is not the critic who counts; not the person who points out how strong persons stumbled or where the doer of deeds could have done them better. The credit belongs to the person who is actually in the arena, whose face is marred by dust, and sweat, and blood; who strives valiantly; who errs and comes short again and again; who knows the great enthusiasms, the great devotions, and spends a life in a worthy cause; who at the best, knows in the end the triumph of high achievement; and who at the worst, if he or she fails, at least fails while daring greatly, so that their place shall never be with those cold and timid souls who knew neither victory nor defeat.

—Theodore Roosevelt

Tom Vilsack was in the arena.

TOM VILSACK is the governor of Iowa.

CHARLES YEAGER

General Charles E. "Chuck" Yeager was born in the hills of West Virginia. From a very early age, he was raised by his father and mother to honor his flag and his country. He enlisted in the Army Air Corps at age eighteen in September 1941, was selected for pilot training in September 1942, trained as a Fighter Pilot, and was sent overseas to England in November 1943 where he flew the first Mustangs in the 8th Air Force.

Yeager was shot down over occupied France in March 1944 and evaded the Germans. There wasn't a German alive that could catch a West Virginian in the woods. He escaped to Spain and, after being traded for gasoline, was flown back to England by the British. Because he was an evadee, the military tried to send him home but he protested all the way up the chain to General Eisenhower, who was astounded by someone who was so insistent on putting himself in harm's way to serve his country. General Eisenhower allowed Yeager to go back to his squadron where he flew fifty-six more combat missions and became a Fighter Ace, shooting down thirteen German airplanes including a jet-powered Me 262. "The first time I saw a jet," he later recalled, "I shot it down."

Yeager always considered combat to be the ultimate flying experience. He became an ace in a day when he shot down five Me 109s on October 12, 1944. But it was a later mission, on November 27, 1944, when he shot down four Focke Wulf 190s that made the most vivid impression on him. "That day was a fighter pilot's dream," he recalled. "In the midst of a wild sky, I knew that dog-fighting was what I was born to do."

Yeager returned home in February of 1945 and was subsequently assigned to Wright Field where he attended Test Pilot School. Although he was the most junior pilot in the Flight Test Division, he was selected to fly the Bell X-1, the nation's first research rocket airplane. He became the first person to fly faster than the speed of sound in that airplane on October 14, 1947. Yeager later flew the Bell X-1A at two and a half times the speed of sound in December 1953.

After nine years at Wright Field and Edwards AFB as a Test Pilot, Yeager served in progressively more responsible positions, including multiple tours as a fighter squadron and wing commander. As commander of the 405th Fighter Wing, he returned to combat, logging 127 missions during the Vietnam conflict. Promoted to Brigadier General in 1969, he concluded his military career with senior-level assignments as vice commander of the Seventh Air Force, U.S. Defense Representative to Pakistan and, finally, as Director of the USAF Inspection and Safety Center.

He retired in 1975 after thirty-four years' active duty and continued to serve as a consulting test pilot at Edwards AFB for the next twenty-eight years. He flew his last official military flight in an F-15E Strike Eagle on October 26, 2002, winding up completing *sixty* years in Air Force cockpits at the age of seventy-nine.

While a consultant, Yeager served on various boards and also participated in many events to raise money for children, aviation, Down's syndrome folks, autistic folks, fish habitat, and college scholarships. He donated much of his own time and money. Yeager also wrote a best-selling autobiography, *Yeager*, and continued to fly, backpack, fish, and hunt until the day he died. At age seventy-nine, he started the General Chuck Yeager Foundation, whose mission was to inspire others to live up to the ideals by which he lived—honor, integrity, duty and service to your country.

Yeager was the recipient of every major award in the field of flight. One such award was the Collier Trophy presented by President Truman, during which ceremony, Yeager's father, a staunch Republican, refused to shake hands with the President. To make up for this, Yeager's mother exchanged cornbread recipes with the President. Another of the awards Yeager received was the only Peacetime Congressional Medal of Honor, presented by President Ford in 1976.

Due to his humility regarding his fame, he never put much stock in labels such as "The Right Stuff." Instead, when asked about his event-filled career, his typical response was: "I was just doing my job." Of all the hundreds of honors and tributes he received, perhaps the most meaningful for him came from former President George Bush when, in congratulating him on the fiftieth anniversary of his flight through the sound barrier, he wrote: "If I was asked to choose one word that would define Chuck Yeager, it would be Service. Fighter pilot, test pilot, combat commander, you have always valued service to our country above all else, Chuck; the courage, resourcefulness, and integrity which you have displayed so magnificently throughout over five decades of service to the United States are the very qualities that built this country into the greatest nation on earth."

He was a genuinely patriotic American who always said, "What I am, I owe to the Air Force."

Instead of flowers, please send donations to the General Chuck Yeager Foundation at P.O. Box 579, Penn Valley, CA 95946 or through General Chuck Yeager's office website: www.generalchuckyeager.com

CHARLES "CHUCK" YEAGER is a retired Air Force brigadier general and the first man to fly faster than the speed of sound.

The
Final
Frontier

SCIENTISTS AND EDUCATORS

PATCH ADAMS

೧೦೦

Don't remember me when I am gone. Remember to serve the causes of peace, justice and care. As Albert Einstein said, "Only a life lived for others is a life worthwhile."

I lecture three hundred days a year all over the world and come with a message for compassion and generosity in action. Then I'm gone, so I'm faced with this remembering when I am gone almost daily. I work hard to crush the experience of awe for fame, saying, "Forget me. Remember the call to service." Having served now almost forty years, I have an opportunity to hear frequently how people felt influenced by me (I hear that they mean influenced by my words and example). I work to be more skilled for a broader diversity of that influence. So I don't care about any eulogy or epitaph; I care every day to see how I can be a better instrument for peace, justice and care while I am alive. If the influence to serve others lives after I die, then happily I'm (the ideas) not gone, and the rememberings are in acts of care.

೧೦೦

PATCH ADAMS is a prominent physician who has helped and healed thousands of ill children. His multiple talents extend far beyond medicine, as he is also a professional clown, a social activist, a performer, and the author of several books on wellness and healing.

BUZZ ALDRIN

❧

Could not, would not give up on space exploration!

❧

BUZZ ALDRIN is a former NASA astronaut. As the lunar module pilot of Apollo XI in July 1969, he and Neil Armstrong were the first humans to walk on the moon.

ROBERT BALLARD

❧

During his life, Bob Ballard came into contact with millions of your children around the world. He always told them to study hard and to follow their dream. Not their parent's dream, not their teacher's dream, but their dream. It is the passion for your dream, he would say, that will get you through life. It will get you back up after life knocks you down.

His grandmother told him when he was growing up, "Great is the person who plants a tree knowing he will never sit in its shade." So Bob Ballard spent his life planting the seeds of curiosity in the minds of children knowing they would bear fruit long after he was gone.

❧

ROBERT D. BALLARD is an underwater explorer and author. His most famous discoveries include the discovery of the *Titanic* and the German battleship *Bismarck*. He founded the Institute for Exploration, which focuses on expanding deep-sea research.

EUGENE CERNAN

∽o∾

As a child, my dream was to fly airplanes and perhaps one day soar into the heavens and go where no man had gone before. To inspire a child to shoot for the moon and remind him that even if he misses, he will land among the stars—this is perhaps the real message to pass on when I'm gone.

∽o∾

EUGENE CERNAN is a former NASA astronaut, a two-time recipient of the NASA Distinguished Service Medal, and an inductee into the U.S. Space Hall of Fame. He has logged more than 550 hours in space, with more than 73 of those hours on the surface of the moon.

DENTON COOLEY

∽o∾

Innovator, educator, family man, friend.
Builder for eternity.

And each must make
Ere life has flown
A stumbling block
Or a stepping stone.

—R. L. Sharpe

∽o∾

DENTON A. COOLEY is a world-renowned heart surgeon and the founder of the Texas Heart Institute. In 1968, he performed the first successful human heart transplant in the United States and a year later was the first heart surgeon to implant an artificial heart. He is also a recipient of the Medal of Freedom, America's highest civilian award.

JOAN EMBERY

∾o∾

The best tribute is having affected the world in a positive way. Therefore I would like to be remembered for my passion for wildlife and encouraging people to value our incredible natural resources. It's what we leave behind that determines our success. What better way to contribute than to leave our natural world intact.

Today we are challenged to determine the fate of animal life on our planet and the delicate balance of natural resources. Decisions we make today will determine the health of our world and the future of all its inhabitants.

We humans have the ability to define our future quality of life and the fate of those without a voice. It has been my life's focus and ambition to encourage people to preserve our natural world and its incredible beauty and diversity and ensure a healthy planet for both humans and animals.

∾o∾

JOAN EMBERY is the Goodwill Ambassador for the Zoological Society of San Diego and the author of four books. She has brought the animal kingdom home to thousands of people through her numerous television appearances and public lectures. She is an adamant environmentalist and animal rights advocate.

JACK HANNA

❧

If I've stirred something inside you that has given you more compassion for the animal kingdom, then I've made my mark in the world.

❧

JACK HANNA is the host of the popular television series *Jack Hanna's Animal Adventures*, widely syndicated and viewed in more than sixty countries. He has been the director emeritus of the Columbus Zoo in Ohio since 1993 and is a professional fellow of the American Zoo and Aquarium Association.

C. EVERETT KOOP

❧

He redefined the office of Surgeon General of the United States and after serving two four-year terms, he remained the health conscience of the nation.

❧

C. EVERETT KOOP is a former U.S. surgeon general. He now serves as senior scholar of the C. Everett Koop Institute at Dartmouth College, created to promote the health and well-being of all people. In addition to receiving a vast number of awards, he is the recipient of thirty-five honorary doctorate degrees.

LAURA SCHLESSINGER

✎∘✎

How arrogant to write your own epitaph!!

✎∘✎

DR. LAURA SCHLESSINGER is a psychologist with a wide fan base from her radio program and television appearances. She has also written popular books such as *Ten Stupid Things Women Do to Mess Up Their Lives* and *Ten Stupid Things Men Do to Mess Up Their Lives.*

ANDREW WEIL

✎∘✎

He helped steer medicine back on course by reconnecting it with nature and refocusing it on health and healing. He encouraged patients to have greater confidence in the body's ability to heal itself and taught physicians to regard treatments as facilitators of intrinsic healing processes. He tried to make his own life a model for wellness and always insisted that total health means health of body, mind, and spirit, not just soundness of the physical body.

✎∘✎

ANDREW WEIL is a widely recognized expert on integrative medicine and the author of eight books, including several national bestsellers.

And finally, the last word from

LARRY KING

I would like to be remembered as a kid from Brooklyn who probably would have preferred to become a first baseman or a pitcher for the Brooklyn Dodgers, but who never made it.

I am, of course, proudest of my kids and madly in love with my wife, Shawn.

But above all, I would like to be remembered as a broadcaster who has perhaps interviewed more people than anyone in history, from kings and queens to presidents, from movie stars to legendary athletes, from writers to Nobel Prize winners, from saints to sinners, I have talked to them all. I am grateful to the listeners who have kept me going all these years, and I hope that fifty years from now when people talk about Larry King, they will say, "He did a *hell* of an interview!"

LARRY KING is a talk-show host.